Daily
Academic Vocabulary

GRADE 5

Editorial Development: Bonnie Brook Communications
Content Editing: Marilyn Evans
Leslie Sorg
Copy Editing: Cathy Harber
Art Direction: Cheryl Puckett
Cover Design: Cheryl Puckett
Illustration: Jim Palmer
Design/Production: Carolina Caird
Arynne Elfenbein

EMC 2761
Visit
teaching-standards.com
to view a correlation
of this book.

Correlated to Current Standards

Congratulations on your purchase of some of the finest teaching materials in the world.

Photocopying the pages in this book is permitted for <u>single-classroom use only</u>. Making photocopies for additional classes or schools is prohibited.

For information about other Evan-Moor products, call 1-800-777-4362, fax 1-800-777-4332, or visit our website, www.evan-moor.com. Entire contents © 2007 Evan-Moor Corporation 10 Harris Court, Suite C-3, Monterey, CA 93940-5773. Printed in USA.

CPSIA: P.A. Hutchison Co., Mayfield, PA, USA [4/2024]

Contents

WEEK		PAGE
1	typical, standard	10
2	suppose, assume, assumption, presume	14
3	convince, persuade, persuasion, persuasive	18
4	imply, implication, contend	22
5	perform, performance, accomplish, accomplishment	26
6	translate, translation, quote, quotation	30
7	interpret, interpretation, clarify	34
8	estimate, estimation, calculate	38
9	review of weeks 1–8	42
10	refer, reference	46
11	specify, specific, detail, in detail	50
12	complicate, complicated, complication, complex	54
13	defend, viewpoint, position, perspective	58
14	assign, assignment, delegate, designate	62
15	apply, application, applicable	66
16	inform, information, evidence, evident	70
17	develop, development	74
18	review of weeks 10–17	78
19	significance, significant, insignificant, emphasis, emphasize	82

WEEK		PAGE
20	condition, factor, aspect	86
21	modify, modification, substitute	90
22	pattern, imitate, imitation	94
23	accurate, accuracy, precise, precision	98
24	primary, dominant, prevalent	102
25	criticism, critique, critical	106
26	address, focus, topic	110
27	review of weeks 19–26	114
28	associate, association, relationship, relative to	118
29	constant, consistent, consistency	122
30	conform, correspond, corresponding, correspondence	126
31	distinct, distinction, differentiate, discriminate	130
32	represent, representative, symbolize, symbol, symbolic	134
33	determine, influence	138
34	respond, response, elaborate	142
35	category, categorize, consist, constitute	146
36	review of weeks 28–35	150
Answer Key		154
Word Index		159
Reproducible Definitions		160

About Academic Vocabulary

What Is Academic Vocabulary?

Academic vocabulary is that critical vocabulary that students meet again and again in their reading and classroom work across all content areas. Feldman and Kinsella refer to these high-use, widely applicable words—words such as *compare, occurrence, structure, sequential, symbolize,* and *inference*—as "academic tool kit words."[1]

Why Is Academic Vocabulary Instruction Important?

Vocabulary knowledge is one of the most reliable predictors of academic success. Studies show a major difference over time between the achievement levels of children who enter school with a strong oral vocabulary and those who begin their schooling with a limited vocabulary. Dr. Anita Archer says, "In many ways the 'Reading Gap,' especially after second and third grades, is essentially a Vocabulary Gap—and the longer students are in school the wider the gap becomes."[2] Focused vocabulary instruction can reduce this gap.

Knowing academic vocabulary—the "vocabulary of learning"—is essential for students to understand concepts presented in school. Yet academic English is not typically part of students' natural language and must be taught. "One of the most crucial services that teachers can provide, particularly for students who do not come from academically advantaged backgrounds, is systematic instruction in important academic terms."[3]

What Does Research Say About Vocabulary Instruction?

Common practices for teaching vocabulary—looking up words in the dictionary, drawing meaning from context, and impromptu instruction—are important but cannot be depended upon alone to develop the language students need for academic success.

Most vocabulary experts recommend a comprehensive vocabulary development program with direct instruction of important words. *Daily Academic Vocabulary* utilizes direct teaching in which students use academic language in speaking, listening, reading, and writing. Used consistently, *Daily Academic Vocabulary* will help students acquire the robust vocabulary necessary for academic success.

[1]Feldman, K., and Kinsella, K. "Narrowing the Language Gap: The Case for Explicit Vocabulary Instruction." New York: Scholastic, 2004.

[2]Archer, A. "Vocabulary Development." Working paper, 2003. (http://www.fcoe.net/ela/pdf/Anita%20Archer031.pdf)

[3]Marzano, R. J. and Pickering, D. J. *Building Academic Vocabulary.* Alexandria, VA: Association for Supervision and Curriculum Development, 2005.

Tips for Successful Vocabulary Teaching

The "Weekly Walk-Through" on pages 6 and 7 presents a suggested instructional path for teaching the words in *Daily Academic Vocabulary*. Here are some ideas from vocabulary experts to ensure that students get the most from these daily lessons.*

Active Participation Techniques

- Active participation means ALL students are speaking and writing.
- Use **choral responses**:
    - Pronounce the word together.
    - Read the sentence/question together.
    - Complete cloze sentences together.
- Use **nonverbal responses**:
    - Students give thumbs-up signal, point to the word, etc.
    - Make sure students wait for your signal to respond.
- Use **partner responses**:
    - Have students practice with a partner first.
    - Listen in on several pairs.
- Allow thinking time before taking responses.
- Randomly call on students; don't ask for raised hands.
- Ask students to rephrase what a partner or other classmate said.

Model and Practice

- Use an oral cloze strategy when discussing a new word. Invite choral responses. For example: *If I read you the end of a story, I am reading you the _____.* (Students say, "conclusion.")
- Complete the open-ended sentence (activity 1 on Days 1–4) yourself before asking students to do so.
- Make a point of using the week's words in your conversation and instruction (both oral and written). Be sure to call students' attention to the words and confirm understanding in each new context.
- Encourage students to look for the week's words as they read content area texts.
- Find moments during the day (waiting in line, in between lessons) to give students additional opportunities to interact with the words. For example:

    *If what I say is an example of **accomplish**, say "accomplish." If what I say is <u>not</u> an example of **accomplish**, show me a thumbs-down sign.*

    > *I meant to clean my room, but I watched TV instead.* (thumbs down)
    > *Stacia read two books a week, more than any other student.* ("accomplish")
    > *The scientists found a cure for the disease.* ("accomplish")
    > *The mechanic could not fix our car.* (thumbs down)

---

* See also page 9 for specific ideas for English language learners.

Each week of *Daily Academic Vocabulary* follows the same five-day format, making the content more accessible for both students and teacher.

Using the reproducible definitions and the teacher lesson plan page, follow the instructional steps below to introduce each day's word or words.

1. **Pronounce** the word and point out the part of speech. Then have students say the word with you several times. If the word is long, pronounce it again by syllables, having students repeat after you.

2. **Read the definition** of the word; paraphrase using simpler or different language if necessary.

3. **Read the example sentence** and then have students read it with you. Discuss how the word is used in the sentence and ask questions to confirm understanding. For example: *We are waiting for a **definite** answer from Aunt Caitlin about when she is coming for a visit.* Ask: *What kind of answer would be a **definite** answer? What kind of answer would not be a **definite** answer?* Provide additional example sentences as necessary.

4. **Elaborate** on the meaning of the word using the suggestions on the teacher lesson plan page. These suggestions draw on common life experiences to illustrate the word meaning and give students opportunities to generate their own examples of use.

Teacher Resources

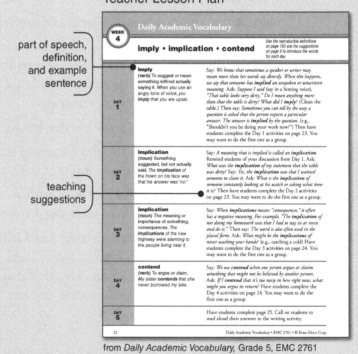

from *Daily Academic Vocabulary*, Grade 5, EMC 2761

Student Practice Pages

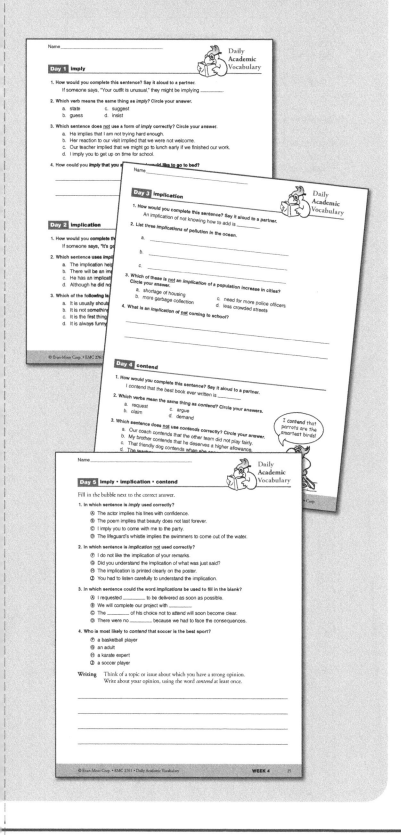

5. **Assess** students' understanding of the word(s) with the reproducible activities for Days 1 through 4.

   The first item is always an oral activity that is designed to be open-ended and answerable based on personal experience. You may wish to model a response before asking students to complete the item. Make sure that all students respond orally. Then call on a number of students to share their responses or those of a partner.

   Until students become familiar with the variety of formats used in the daily practice, you may wish to do the activities together as a class. This will provide support for English language learners and struggling readers.

6. **Review and assess** mastery of all the words from the week on Day 5. The review contains four multiple-choice items and a writing activity requiring students to use one or more of the week's words.

The instructional steps above were modeled after those presented by Kevin Feldman, Ed.D. and Kate Kinsella, Ed.D. in "Narrowing the Language Gap: The Case for Explicit Vocabulary Instruction," Scholastic Inc., 2004.

Review Week Walk-Through

Weeks 9, 18, 27, and 36 are review weeks. Each review covers all the words from the previous eight weeks.

Days 1–4

On Day 1 through Day 4 of the review weeks, students determine which academic vocabulary words complete a cloze paragraph.

Day 5

Day 5 of the review weeks alternates between a crossword puzzle and a crack-the-code puzzle.

Teacher Page

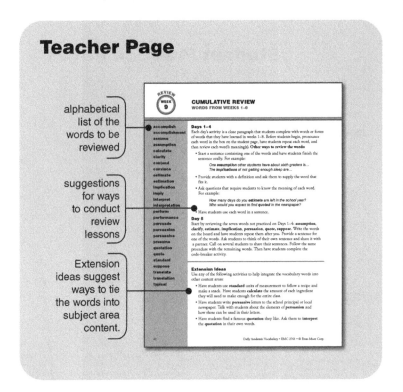

alphabetical list of the words to be reviewed

suggestions for ways to conduct review lessons

Extension ideas suggest ways to tie the words into subject area content.

Student Practice Pages

Days 1–4

Day 5

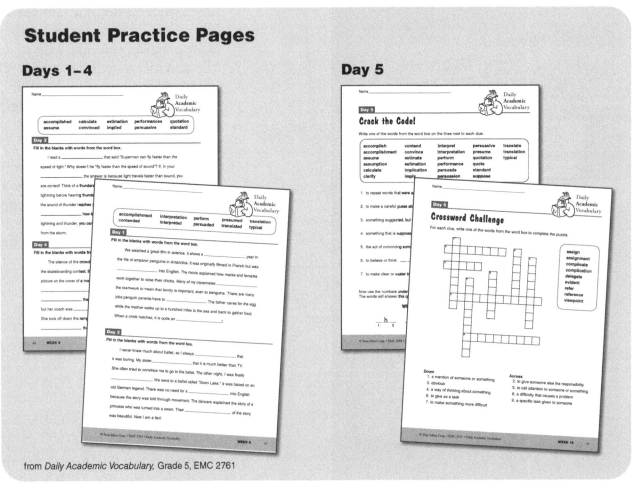

from *Daily Academic Vocabulary*, Grade 5, EMC 2761

In addition to the direct, scaffolded instruction presented in *Daily Academic Vocabulary,* you may want to use some of the following sheltering strategies to assist English language learners in accessing the vocabulary.

Use Graphics
Draw a picture, a symbol, or other graphics such as word or idea maps to represent the word. Keep it simple. Then ask students to draw their own pictures. For example:

| categorize | similar |

Use Cognates with Spanish-Speaking Students
Cognates—words that are similar in meaning, spelling, and pronunciation—can make English more accessible for Spanish speakers. There are thousands of English words that have a related Spanish word. For example:

typical	típico
variety	variedad
combination	combinación

Model Correct Syntax and Usage in Oral Discussions
Model correct pronunciation. Use echoing strategies to teach correct usage and syntax. Teach the varied forms of words together, *agree* and *agreement* for example, to help students understand correct usage.

Provide Sentence Frames
For written activities, such as the final activity on all Day 5 pages, provide sentence starters or sentence frames that students can complete. For example:

*We knew that our study method was **effective** because…*

Teach Communication Strategies
Engaging in academic discussions requires a more formal language. Teach a variety of ways to begin responses when reporting or asking questions in class. For example:

Change this	To this
My partner said…	My partner shared/pointed out/indicated that…
That's not right!	I don't agree with you because…
I don't get it.	Will you explain that to me again?

typical • standard

Use the reproducible definitions on page 160 and the suggestions on page 6 to introduce the words for each day.

DAY 1

typical
(adj.) Showing the traits or characteristics that are normal for a certain thing. *Yesterday was a typical school day.*

Say: *When something is typical, it has the traits or characteristics that we expect it to have. Typical can be used to describe many kinds of things. It might describe a person, an animal, or an object.* Ask: *How would you describe a typical city?* (e.g., large; exciting; noisy) *How would you describe a typical firefighter?* (e.g., brave; strong) Then have students complete the Day 1 activities on page 11. You may want to do the first one as a group.

DAY 2

standard
(adj.) Normal or regular; typical. *"Hello" is the standard greeting on the telephone.*

Say: *Standard and "typical" are synonyms; they have about the same meaning. Often, one can be substituted for the other.* Ask students to consider some examples. Say: *The standard school bus is yellow. The standard plate is round.* Have volunteers substitute "typical" for **standard** in the examples and ask the class if the meaning of the sentence changes. Then have students complete the Day 2 activities on page 11. You may want to do the first one as a group.

DAY 3

standard
(noun) A model or example used to determine how good other things are. *Our best player's kicking sets a high standard for the rest of the team.*

Say: *To judge the quality of something—perhaps a painting, a performance, or schoolwork—we might compare it to a good example of what we are judging. That good example is the standard.* Ask: *What is the best book you have ever read?* Say: *This book sets the standard by which you judge all other books.* Then have students complete the Day 3 activities on page 12. You may want to do the first one as a group.

DAY 4

standard
(adj.) Widely accepted as a rule or model. *The standard procedure for a fire drill requires us to move quickly and quietly.*

Explain that for something to be considered **standard**, people must agree that it meets certain requirements. Say: *You should always use a standard dictionary to check your spelling. A standard dictionary has been reviewed and approved by many people.* Point out that things we do are also considered **standard** when there are widely accepted ways of how to do them. Say: *A standard way to brush your teeth is in small circles, front to back.* Then have students complete the Day 4 activities on page 12. You may want to do the first one as a group.

DAY 5

Have students complete page 13. Call on students to read aloud their answers to the writing activity.

Name_____

Day 1 typical

1. How would you complete this sentence? Say it aloud to a partner.

My typical breakfast includes _____.

2. What do you do on a *typical* weekend? List three activities.

a. _____

b. _____

c. _____

3. Which ingredients might be included in a *typical* sandwich? Circle your answers.

a. cheese   c. mustard

b. watermelon   d. cereal

Day 2 standard

1. How would you complete this sentence? Say it aloud to a partner.

In a standard classroom, you will find _____.

2. Which word means the same as *standard*? Circle your answer.

a. boring   c. awful

b. special   d. typical

3. List three parts of a *standard* bicycle.

a. _____

b. _____

c. _____

4. What is your *standard* bedtime?

_____

Daily
Academic
Vocabulary

Day 3 standard

1. **How would you complete these sentences? Say them aloud to a partner.**

   The person I admire most is _____. This person sets the standard
   for a hero by _____.

2. **Which of these people sets the *standard* for a baseball team? Circle your answer.**

   a. the player who scores the most runs

   b. the coach who decides the plays

   c. the player who always strikes out

   d. the umpire who rules on the plays

3. **What qualities might describe a student who sets a high *standard* of excellence?**
   Circle your answers.

   a. always checks his or her work

   b. always checks the clock to see when class will be over

   c. always asks questions when he or she doesn't understand something

   d. always tries to be first to finish eating at lunchtime

4. **What would you like to set the *standard* for?**

   _____

Day 4 standard

1. **How would you complete this sentence? Say it aloud to a partner.**

   Standard safety rules for riding your bicycle include _____.

2. **Which of the following are *standard* reference books that you would find**
   in your school library? Circle your answers.

   a. car repair manual

   b. dictionary

   c. encyclopedia

   d. cookbook

3. **List three positive examples of *standard* classroom behavior.**

   a. _____

   b. _____

   c. _____

Name_____

Day 5 typical • standard

Fill in the bubble next to the correct answer.

1. Which sentence uses the word *typical* correctly?

Ⓐ I chose this typical shirt because it was different.

Ⓑ A typical school lunch includes milk.

Ⓒ That typical ice cream was the best I've ever eaten.

Ⓓ That huge, record-breaking storm on Tuesday was typical.

2. Which of the following is <u>not</u> *standard* behavior for a cat?

Ⓕ eating

Ⓖ purring

Ⓗ barking

Ⓙ licking

3. Which of these workers do <u>not</u> set a high *standard* for bravery?

Ⓐ firefighters

Ⓑ lifeguards

Ⓒ circus clowns

Ⓓ police officers

4. Which of the following books is a *standard* reference book?

Ⓕ *Stuart Little*

Ⓖ *Webster's Dictionary*

Ⓗ *The Life and Times of Abe Lincoln*

Ⓙ *The Secret of the Old Clock*

Writing   Think of a famous athlete, artist, actor, writer, or scientist and tell how he or she has set a high *standard* of performance for other people. Use the word *standard* in your writing.

_____

_____

_____

_____

suppose • assume
assumption • presume

Use the reproducible definitions on page 161 and the suggestions on page 6 to introduce the words for each day.

DAY 1

suppose
(verb) To believe; to think. *I suppose that I could do better on tests if I studied more.*

Tell students that we use the verb **suppose** when we are reasonably, but not positively, sure of something. Say: *For instance, because you are good students, I suppose that you will complete your homework assignments on time.* Then have students complete the Day 1 activities on page 15. You may want to do the first one as a group.

DAY 2

assume
(verb) To take a duty, job, or responsibility upon yourself. *As an older brother, I always assume the responsibility of watching out for my younger sister.*

Tell students that **assume** can mean "to take on." Say: *When you take on or assume a task or role, you also assume or take on the responsibilities and duties that go with it.* Discuss the responsibilities a student might **assume** if he or she were asked to lead a group of first-graders to the library. Then have students complete the Day 2 activities on page 15. You may want to do the first one as a group.

DAY 3

assume
(verb) To suppose that something is right without checking it. *I assume we will practice on Saturday.*

assumption
(noun) Something that is supposed, expected, or taken for granted. *My assumption is that the story will have a happy ending.*

Tell students that to **assume** can also mean to think that something is true without finding out for sure. Say: *Sometimes you can be wrong when you assume something. For example, you might assume that you have practice on Saturday. Because you usually have practice on Saturday, you don't feel that it's necessary to check the schedule. You make the assumption that the schedule has not changed.* Explain that when we **assume**, we make an **assumption**. Then have students complete the Day 3 activities on page 16. You may want to do the first one as a group.

DAY 4

presume
(verb) To think that something is true without really knowing or having all the facts. *A jury must presume that defendants are innocent until evidence proves them guilty.*

Say: *"Assume" and presume are synonyms.* Then ask: *What is something you think is true, or presume, about monkeys?* (e.g., eat bananas; live in trees) *Now, do you know those things for a fact? Do you know everything about monkeys?* After students reply, say: *No. We are not experts on monkeys. Therefore, we presume some of the things we know about them. We don't know for a fact that everything we think about them is true.* Ask: *Can you think of other information we presume about animals?* Then have students complete the Day 4 activities on page 16. You may want to do the first one as a group.

DAY 5

Have students complete page 17. Call on students to read aloud their answers to the writing activity.

Daily Academic Vocabulary

Day 1 suppose

1. How would you complete this sentence? Say it aloud to a partner.

If I could travel anywhere I wanted, I suppose I would first go to _____.

2. Which sentence does not use *suppose* correctly? Circle your answer.

    a. Karen supposed that she would be invited to her friend's party.

    b. I asked Sam because he always supposes the answer.

    c. I suppose the movie will be about two hours long.

    d. Do you suppose I should take my umbrella?

3. Which word means the same thing as *suppose?* Circle your answer.

    a. want   c. know

    b. appreciated   d. think

4. What do you *suppose* will happen next in a book you are reading?

_____

_____

Day 2 assume

1. How would you complete this sentence? Say it aloud to a partner.

At home, I assume responsibility for _____.

2. Which sentence does not use *assume* correctly? Circle your answer.

    a. The new teacher will assume the role of lunch monitor.

    b. Todd has assumed responsibility for feeding the dog.

    c. That boy assumed too much pizza.

    d. Ms. Kline will assume the job of coach for our team.

3. Match the people below with one of the duties that they *assume* in their jobs. Write the correct letter on the line.

___ boat captain   a. to make sure that trials are fair

___ mayor   b. to do things to make the city a better place

___ judge   c. to help sick people get better

___ doctor   d. to make sure the crew and passengers are safe

Name_____

Day 3 assume • assumption

1. How would you complete these sentences? Say them aloud to a partner.

Our teacher assumes that we know _____.

Every school day I make the assumption that _____.

2. Which of these words is a synonym for *assume*? Circle your answer.

a. agree   c. wonder

b. create   d. suppose

3. Which of these statements is true? Circle your answer.

a. When we make an assumption, we can be sure that we're right.

b. When we make an assumption, we might be right or we might be wrong.

c. When we make an assumption, we can be sure that we're wrong.

d. When we make an assumption, no one will agree with us.

4. What is an *assumption* you have about being an adult?

_____

_____

Day 4 presume

1. How would you complete this sentence? Say it aloud to a partner.

I can presume that I am always welcome to visit at _____.

What do you **presume** about parrots?

2. Which sentence uses the word *presume* correctly? Circle your answer.

a. I presume about going on vacation.

b. Since I studied for the test, I presumed all of the correct answers.

c. When I go to see a movie, I presume that I will enjoy it.

d. Judy presumes a new computer for her birthday.

3. Which of the following might you most likely *presume*? Circle your answer.

a. that you will improve your work by checking it

b. that everything you read in a fairy tale is true

c. that your best friend will forget your name

d. that you will see many paintings and sculptures at the science museum

Name_____

Day 5 **suppose • assume • assumption • presume**

Fill in the bubble next to the correct answer.

1. Which sentence uses the word *suppose* correctly?

Ⓐ I supposed all of the answers on the test.

Ⓑ Felicia supposed the definition for the word in the dictionary.

Ⓒ Dad supposed that the turkey was fully cooked when the timer went off.

Ⓓ Last night, I supposed about a new bike.

2. Which sentence does not use the word *assume* correctly?

Ⓕ We assume that the school bus will be on time every day.

Ⓖ Jamie assumes responsibility for turning in his homework on time.

Ⓗ My uncle will assume the position of fire chief next week.

Ⓙ The mayor assumes her lunch at noon every day.

3. Which sentence is not a reasonable *assumption*?

Ⓐ The sun will rise in the morning.

Ⓑ A student who studies hard will learn more than one who does not.

Ⓒ The sun will rise in the evening.

Ⓓ My alarm clock will wake me up if I set it correctly.

4. What could you *presume* about a book that all your friends like?

Ⓕ that you will hate it

Ⓖ that you should not read it

Ⓗ that you will also like it

Ⓙ that it will make you laugh

Writing   What do you *suppose* a book entitled *Flying to the Moon: My Adventures in the Space Program* would be about? What *assumptions* could you make about the author's background? Use at least one of this week's words.

_____

_____

_____

_____

Daily Academic Vocabulary

convince • persuade
persuasion • persuasive

Use the reproducible definitions on page 162 and the suggestions on page 6 to introduce the words for each day.

DAY 1

convince
(verb) To make someone believe or accept something. *Raul **convinced** me to choose him as president of our gamers club.*

Say: *If you **convince** someone, you get the person to believe you or do what you want. That may involve getting the person to change his or her mind.* Relate a time when you were **convinced** about something, such as: *I never liked yellow cars until the salesperson **convinced** me that the color would make me feel happy and cheerful.* Ask students to describe instances when someone tried to **convince** them or they tried to **convince** someone. Then have students complete the Day 1 activities on page 19. You may want to do the first one as a group.

DAY 2

persuade
(verb) To convince someone to do or believe something. *Please **persuade** your sister to wear a raincoat today.*

Say: ***Persuade** and "convince" are synonyms. When we **persuade** someone, we get them to do or believe something. For example, I could **persuade** all of you to be very quiet if I promised you extra recess. I could convince you to act a certain way.* Then ask students to talk about what they do or say when they want to **persuade** someone to do something for them. Ask: *What is the difference between trying to **persuade** someone to do or believe something and trying to force a person to do or believe something?* Then have students complete the Day 2 activities on page 19. You may want to do the first one as a group.

DAY 3

persuasion
(noun) The act of convincing; the ability to convince someone to do or believe something. *A good salesperson has strong skills of **persuasion**.*

Say: *Think about yesterday's discussion. I offered you something like (extra recess) in order to persuade you. That was my form of **persuasion**.* Ask: *What other methods or forms of **persuasion** have you used, experienced, or seen on TV? How do people try to persuade you to do things?* Encourage students to use the word **persuasion** in their responses. Then have students complete the Day 3 activities on page 20. You may want to do the first one as a group.

DAY 4

persuasive
(adj.) Having the ability to cause someone to do or believe something. *Her **persuasive** speech convinced us to vote for her.*

Say: *If someone is able to persuade someone else, they are **persuasive**.* Ask: *Do you know any **persuasive** people? What makes them **persuasive**?* Encourage students to use the word **persuasive** in their responses. Then have students complete the Day 4 activities on page 20. You may want to do the first one as a group.

DAY 5

Have students complete page 21. Call on students to read aloud their answers to the writing activity.

Name _____

Day 1   convince

1. How would you complete this sentence? Say it aloud to a partner.

I think I could convince my friend to _____.

2. Which sentence shows that someone was *convinced*? Circle your answer.

    a. Dad would not let me trade walking the dog for doing the dishes.

    b. The team decided to practice for one hour.

    c. Clarissa agreed to help me after I explained how much I needed her help.

    d. I was the only one in class who did not like the story.

3. Which sentences use the word *convince* correctly? Circle your answers.

    a. I can't convince how the magician did that trick.

    b. The lawyer must convince the jury to vote in favor of her client.

    c. Will you convince me if I promise to tell you a secret?

    d. Do you think his friends can convince him to try out for the play?

Day 2   persuade

1. How would you complete this sentence? Say it aloud to a partner.

I would like to persuade my parents to let me _____.

2. Which phrase best completes this sentence? Circle your answer.

If I wanted to persuade my friend to lend me a favorite book, I would promise _____.

    a. to treat it with care   c. to rip out only a few pages

    b. not to read it   d. to draw funny pictures in it

3. What are three ways to *persuade* someone to do something?

    a. _____

    b. _____

    c. _____

4. What is something you were once *persuaded* to do?

_____

_____

Day 3 | persuasion

1. How would you complete this sentence? Say it aloud to a partner.

The last time I used my powers of persuasion, I _____.

2. Which of the following could be part of a successful act of *persuasion*? Circle your answers.

   a. presenting facts
   b. rudeness
   c. politeness
   d. name calling

3. Which sentence shows an act of *persuasion*? Circle your answer.

   a. The girls argued about a color for their room.
   b. Maria's friends told her she had won the contest.
   c. By explaining their ideas, the students convinced the school to serve salads.
   d. Katya begged her teacher to take the class on a field trip.

4. What is a form of *persuasion* you have used?

_____

Day 4 | persuasive

1. How would you complete this sentence? Say it aloud to a partner.

The most persuasive person I know is _____.

2. In which sentence is the word *persuasive* used correctly? Circle your answer.

   a. The roast beef was a persuasive dinner.
   b. The persuasive car was the fastest on the racetrack.
   c. In a persuasive way, Brenda left her book at school.
   d. His reasons for walking instead of taking the bus are persuasive.

3. List three qualities a *persuasive* person might have.

   a. _____

   b. _____

   c. _____

Name_____

Daily Academic Vocabulary

Fill in the bubble next to the correct answer.

1. Which of these best explains the meaning of *convince*?

Ⓐ pout until you get your way

Ⓑ order a person to do what you want

Ⓒ ask nicely, but then yell if the answer is "no"

Ⓓ talk a person into doing what you want

2. Which sentence does <u>not</u> use *persuaded* correctly?

Ⓕ My uncle persuaded me to try out for the team.

Ⓖ Ann persuaded when she heard the sad story.

Ⓗ Dr. Alvarez persuaded his patient to exercise more.

Ⓙ The evidence persuaded the jury that the man was guilty.

> Could I **persuade** you to scratch my back?

3. Which of the following sentences is an example of *persuasion*?

Ⓐ The eggs will hatch in three days.

Ⓑ Did you see the sunset this evening?

Ⓒ You should eat vegetables because they will make you healthier.

Ⓓ Kelley was wearing a pretty dress at the party.

4. Which sentence does <u>not</u> use *persuasive* correctly?

Ⓕ I was so persuasive that nobody believed me.

Ⓖ Our teacher's reasons for giving us the homework were persuasive.

Ⓗ He delivered a persuasive speech in favor of changing the law.

Ⓙ Our dog's loud barking was persuasive, so we took him on his walk.

Writing   Write about a time when you *persuaded* someone to do something or to think about something in a certain way. What made your argument *persuasive?* Use at least two of this week's words in your writing.

_____

_____

_____

_____

imply • implication • contend

Use the reproducible definitions on page 163 and the suggestions on page 6 to introduce the words for each day.

DAY 1

imply
(verb) To suggest or mean something without actually saying it. *When you use an angry tone of voice, you* **imply** *that you are upset.*

Say: *We know that sometimes a speaker or writer may mean more than her words say directly. When this happens, we say that someone has* **implied** *an unspoken or unwritten meaning.* Ask: *Suppose I said* (say in a hinting voice), *"That table looks very dirty." Do I mean anything more than that the table is dirty? What did I* **imply***?* (Clean the table.) Then say: *Sometimes you can tell by the way a question is asked that the person expects a particular answer. The answer is* **implied** *by the question.* (e.g., "Shouldn't you be doing your work now?") Then have students complete the Day 1 activities on page 23. You may want to do the first one as a group.

DAY 2

implication
(noun) Something suggested, but not actually said. *The* **implication** *of the frown on his face was that his answer was "no."*

Say: *A meaning that is implied is called an* **implication***.* Remind students of your discussion from Day 1. Ask: *What was the* **implication** *of my statement that the table was dirty?* Say: *Yes, the* **implication** *was that I wanted someone to clean it.* Ask: *What is the* **implication** *of someone constantly looking at his watch or asking what time it is?* Then have students complete the Day 2 activities on page 23. You may want to do the first one as a group.

DAY 3

implication
(noun) The meaning or importance of something; consequences. *The* **implications** *of the new highway were alarming to the people living near it.*

Say: *When* **implications** *means "consequences," it often has a negative meaning. For example, "The* **implication** *of not doing my homework was that I had to stay in at recess and do it."* Then say: *The word is also often used in the plural form.* Ask: *What might be the* **implications** *of never washing your hands?* (e.g., catching a cold) Have students complete the Day 3 activities on page 24. You may want to do the first one as a group.

DAY 4

contend
(verb) To argue or claim. *My sister* **contends** *that she never borrowed my bike.*

Say: *We use* **contend** *when one person argues or claims something that might not be believed by another person.* Ask: *If I* **contend** *that it's too noisy in here right now, what might you argue in return?* Have students complete the Day 4 activities on page 24. You may want to do the first one as a group.

DAY 5

Have students complete page 25. Call on students to read aloud their answers to the writing activity.

Daily
Academic
Vocabulary

Day 1 imply

1. How would you complete this sentence? Say it aloud to a partner.

If someone says, "Your outfit is unusual," they might be implying _____.

2. Which verb means the same thing as *imply*? Circle your answer.

   a. state   c. suggest
   b. guess   d. insist

3. Which sentence does <u>not</u> use a form of *imply* correctly? Circle your answer.

   a. He implies that I am not trying hard enough.
   b. Her reaction to our visit implied that we were not welcome.
   c. Our teacher implied that we might go to lunch early if we finished our work.
   d. I imply you to get up on time for school.

4. How could you *imply* that you are tired and would like to go to bed?

_____

_____

Day 2 implication

1. How would you complete this sentence? Say it aloud to a partner.

If someone says, "It's getting very loud in here," the implication might be _____.

2. Which sentence uses *implication* correctly? Circle your answer.

   a. The implication helps him drive his truck.
   b. There will be an implication on the exam.
   c. He has an implication that should help him.
   d. Although he did not say it directly, I understood his implication.

3. Which of the following is always true about an *implication*? Circle your answer.

   a. It is usually shouted.
   b. It is not something said directly.
   c. It is the first thing a speaker says.
   d. It is always funny.

Daily Academic Vocabulary

Day 3 | implication

1. How would you complete this sentence? Say it aloud to a partner.

An implication of not knowing how to add is _____.

2. List three *implications* of pollution in the ocean.

a. _____

b. _____

c. _____

3. Which of these is <u>not</u> an *implication* of a population increase in cities? Circle your answer.

a. shortage of housing
b. more garbage collection
c. need for more police officers
d. less crowded streets

4. What is an *implication* of <u>not</u> coming to school?

_____

_____

Day 4 | contend

1. How would you complete this sentence? Say it aloud to a partner.

I contend that the best book ever written is _____.

2. Which verbs mean the same thing as *contend*? Circle your answers.

a. request
b. claim
c. argue
d. demand

3. Which sentence does <u>not</u> use *contends* correctly? Circle your answer.

a. Our coach contends that the other team did not play fairly.
b. My brother contends that he deserves a higher allowance.
c. That friendly dog contends when she sees me.
d. The teacher contends that history is a fun subject to study.

I contend that parrots are the smartest birds!

Daily Academic Vocabulary

Day 5 imply • implication • contend

Fill in the bubble next to the correct answer.

1. In which sentence is *imply* used correctly?

Ⓐ The actor implies his lines with confidence.

Ⓑ The poem implies that beauty does not last forever.

Ⓒ I imply you to come with me to the party.

Ⓓ The lifeguard's whistle implies the swimmers to come out of the water.

2. In which sentence is *implication* <u>not</u> used correctly?

Ⓕ I do not like the implication of your remarks.

Ⓖ Did you understand the implication of what was just said?

Ⓗ The implication is printed clearly on the poster.

Ⓙ You had to listen carefully to understand the implication.

3. In which sentence could the word *implications* be used to fill in the blank?

Ⓐ I requested _____ to be delivered as soon as possible.

Ⓑ We will complete our project with _____.

Ⓒ The _____ of his choice not to attend will soon become clear.

Ⓓ There were no _____ because we had to face the consequences.

4. Who is most likely to *contend* that soccer is the best sport?

Ⓕ a basketball player

Ⓖ an adult

Ⓗ a karate expert

Ⓙ a soccer player

Writing   Think of a topic or issue about which you have a strong opinion. Write about your opinion, using the word *contend* at least once.

_____

_____

_____

_____

perform • performance
accomplish • accomplishment

Use the reproducible definitions on page 164 and the suggestions on page 6 to introduce the words for each day.

DAY 1

perform
(verb) To carry out or do something. *Planning the day's activities is one task that schoolteachers perform.*

Tell students that although we often use the verb **perform** to talk about what someone does to entertain (e.g., **perform** in a play; **perform** a new song), the word has a broader use. Say: *We can also say that the surgeon performed an operation, or that the race car performed well on the track.* Invite students to suggest other examples. Then have students complete the Day 1 activities on page 27. You may want to do the first one as a group.

DAY 2

performance
(noun) The way in which a job or action is carried out. *A test can be used to measure the performance of the students in the class.*

Say: *When we perform a task, the way in which we do the task* (e.g., slowly; carefully) *is our performance.* Say: *An employer might say to an employee, "Your job performance is outstanding, so you will be receiving a raise in pay."* Ask students to use **performance** in sentences relating to other situations. Then have students complete the Day 2 activities on page 27. You may want to do the first one as a group.

DAY 3

accomplish
(verb) To carry out or do something successfully. *I hope to accomplish many things today.*

Tell students that to **accomplish** something is to successfully complete it. Say: *We might ask ourselves, "What did I accomplish today?" Or, "What will I accomplish this year?"* Ask students what they would like to **accomplish** in the next week, having them answer using the sentence starter, "I would like to **accomplish** ___." Then have students complete the Day 3 activities on page 28. You may want to do the first one as a group.

DAY 4

accomplishment
(noun) Something that has been done successfully. *Your perfect score on the test was a great accomplishment.*

Tell students that the suffix "-ment" can turn a verb into a noun, as it does here with the verb "accomplish." Say: *An accomplishment is the thing that has been successfully done.* Have volunteers name one **accomplishment** in their lives so far. Encourage them to use the word **accomplishment** in their responses. Then have students complete the Day 4 activities on page 28. You may want to do the first one as a group.

DAY 5

Have students complete page 29. Call on students to read aloud their answers to the writing activity.

Daily Academic Vocabulary

Day 1 perform

1. How would you complete this sentence? Say it aloud to a partner.

When I perform well on a test, I feel _____.

2. Who is most likely to *perform* an experiment in a lab? Circle your answer.

a. a dog trainer
b. a builder
c. a scientist
d. a chef

3. Which sentence does <u>not</u> use *perform* correctly? Circle your answer.

a. Service dogs can perform basic tasks for their owners.
b. This watch does not perform as advertised.
c. The mayor will perform her duties to her best ability.
d. Tarik was able to perform the movie and told us he liked it.

4. What duties do you *perform* at home?

_____

_____

Day 2 performance

1. How would you complete this sentence? Say it aloud to a partner.

I was most proud of my performance in school when I _____.

2. What can a student do to improve his or her *performance* at school? List three examples.

a. _____

b. _____

c. _____

3. Who will evaluate your *performance* in school and assign a grade to it? Circle your answer.

a. your aunt
b. your school principal
c. your doctor
d. your teacher

Day 3 accomplish

1. How would you complete this sentence? Say it aloud to a partner.

Every week I accomplish the task of _____.

2. Which sentence uses *accomplish* correctly? Circle your answer.

a. In the accomplish of the task, he broke his arm.

b. What do you plan to accomplish today?

c. Jacob had to accomplish his sister to the store.

d. If I accomplish the task, I will still need to finish the task.

3. Which of the following would <u>not</u> help you *accomplish* an athletic feat? Circle your answer.

a. a healthy diet

b. practice

c. too little sleep

d. a good coach

Day 4 accomplishment

1. How would you complete this sentence? Say it aloud to a partner.

One of my accomplishments this week has been _____.

2. List three *accomplishments* that might happen in sports.

a. _____

b. _____

c. _____

3. Which of these sentences does <u>not</u> use *accomplishment* correctly? Circle your answer.

a. In the accomplishment, I am often very worried.

b. He felt that winning the big race was his greatest sports accomplishment.

c. Her accomplishments include climbing Mt. Everest.

d. The students' accomplishments have made their principal proud.

4. Describe your greatest *accomplishment*.

_____

_____

Name _____

Fill in the bubble next to the correct answer.

1. Which of the following sentences does <u>not</u> use *perform* correctly?

Ⓐ Can you perform the task of setting the table?

Ⓑ The perform of the team was not as good as the coach had hoped for.

Ⓒ My older brother performs all of the cooking on Saturdays.

Ⓓ Getting more sleep at night will help me perform better at school.

2. Which sentence uses *performance* correctly?

Ⓕ The judges gave each skater's performance a score from 1 to 10.

Ⓖ When I performance on tests, I get nervous.

Ⓗ The student performances in all areas very well.

Ⓙ Lily received no score because she did not performance.

3. Which task is someone most likely to *accomplish* in one day?

Ⓐ bicycling to a faraway city

Ⓑ cleaning a room

Ⓒ building a house

Ⓓ writing a book

4. Which statement about a "great *accomplishment*" would <u>not</u> be true?

Ⓕ Discovering a cure for a disease would be a great accomplishment.

Ⓖ Sending the first astronaut to the moon was a great accomplishment.

Ⓗ Discovering that our homework is due tomorrow was a great accomplishment.

Ⓙ The invention of the airplane was a great accomplishment.

Writing   Describe something you hope to *accomplish* before the end of this school year. Use at least two of this week's words in your writing.

_____

_____

_____

_____

WEEK 6

translate • translation
quote • quotation

Use the reproducible definitions on page 165 and the suggestions on page 6 to introduce the words for each day.

DAY 1

translate
(verb) To say in another language or change into other words. *I will **translate** my friend's words from Spanish into English for him.*

Say: *To **translate** speech or writing from one language to another requires knowledge of both languages.* Invite any bilingual student in the class to talk about the experience of **translating**. Then say: *We can also **translate** something said in a complicated way into words that are easier to understand.* Write on the board: "My feline companion is enamored of pursuing small, furry rodents." Ask for volunteers to **translate** the sentence into a simpler form. ("My cat likes to chase mice.") Then have students complete the Day 1 activities on page 31. You may want to do the first one as a group.

DAY 2

translation
(noun) A changing of something from one language to another. *Our class read an English **translation** of the original French story.*

Say: *When someone translates a speech or a piece of writing into another language, the result is a **translation**.* If you have access to a bilingual story or book, display it to students. Say: *This book is in both English and (other language). The original (story or book) was written in one language, and then someone did a **translation** of it into the other language.* Then have students complete the Day 2 activities on page 31. You may want to do the first one as a group.

DAY 3

quote
(verb) To repeat words that were spoken or written by someone else. *Mr. Sanchez will often **quote** passages from his favorite poems.*

Bring in a newspaper or magazine article that contains quotations that would be of interest to students. Say: *In this article the reporter **quotes** someone. The report repeats exactly what was said.* Read from the article, then ask: *Who did the reporter **quote**?* Then have students complete the Day 3 activities on page 32. You may want to do the first one as a group.

DAY 4

quotation
(noun) Words that are repeated exactly as spoken or written by someone else. *A **quotation** from the mayor appeared on the front page of the paper.*

Quote a famous poem or phrase that the students will know and ask them whose words you are quoting. (e.g., "I have a dream."—Martin Luther King) Say: *That is a **quotation**.* Then ask students if they can repeat any **quotations** by either a real person or a fictional character in a book or movie. Then have students complete the Day 4 activities on page 32. You may want to do the first one as a group.

DAY 5

Have students complete page 33. Call on students to read aloud their answers to the writing activity.

Daily Academic Vocabulary • EMC 2761 • © Evan-Moor Corporation

Name_____

Day 1 translate

1. How would you complete this sentence? Say it aloud to a partner.

To translate a speech from one language to another, you need to know _____.

2. Which sentence does not use *translate* correctly? Circle your answer.

   a. Our teacher translated the scientist's words into words we could understand.
   b. Mr. Nabokov translates the Russian ambassador's speeches into English.
   c. I wish there was a translate of this book.
   d. Junko translates the lawyer's words into Japanese for her grandfather.

3. Which of the following means the same thing as *translate*? Circle your answer.

   a. change into other words
   b. add more words
   c. invent a new language
   d. work in another country

4. Describe a time when you had to *translate* something.

_____

_____

Day 2 translation

1. How would you complete this sentence? Say it aloud to a partner.

An incorrect translation might cause _____.

2. If you wanted to do *translations* as a job, what would you need to study? Circle your answer.

   a. art and music
   b. languages
   c. mathematics
   d. science

3. Which sentence uses *translation* correctly? Circle your answer.

   a. The tourists turned to their guide for a translation of the man's words.
   b. In the morning, a translation in the traffic can cause a backup.
   c. Translation underwater is helped by having an extra air tank.
   d. If you translation correctly, you will be understood.

Name_____

Day 3   quote

1. How would you complete this sentence? Say it aloud to a partner.

If I could quote one thing my teacher often says, it would be "_____."

2. Which word means the same as *quote*? Circle your answer.

    a. emphasize   c. repeat

    b. allow   d. lie

3. Which of these steps would you <u>not</u> need to take to *quote* someone accurately? Circle your answer.

    a. listen or read carefully

    b. choose different words

    c. double-check your information

    d. proofread your work

4. Why do people *quote* other people?

_____

_____

Day 4   quotation

1. How would you complete this sentence? Say it aloud to a partner.

A quotation that I can remember reading or hearing is "_____."

2. Where would you <u>not</u> be likely to read or hear a *quotation*? Circle your answer.

    a. on a TV newscast

    b. in a book of speeches

    c. in an instruction manual for putting together a toy

    d. in a news magazine

3. Which sentences use *quotation* correctly? Circle your answers.

    a. There was a quotation from the coach's speech in the story about the game.

    b. I used a quotation from an expert on space travel in my report.

    c. The food served at the quotation was very good.

    d. Jordan always likes to quotation his father.

Daily Academic Vocabulary

Day 5 translate • translation • quote • quotation

Fill in the bubble next to the correct answer.

1. Which sentence uses *translate* correctly?

Ⓐ The translate appeared at the bottom of the screen.

Ⓑ Hoy's grandmother can translate anything from Chinese into English.

Ⓒ The chef can translate the most interesting meals.

Ⓓ I took a translate flight to Paris, France.

2. Which of the following is <u>not</u> an example of *translation*?

Ⓕ *Guten Tag* means "Good day" in German.

Ⓖ "Loitering is prohibited" means that hanging around is not allowed.

Ⓗ When we say something is "awesome," we mean that it's really great.

Ⓙ The museum guard said, "Do not touch the paintings."

3. Which source would your teacher be most likely to *quote* when talking about what is happening in the world?

Ⓐ a comic book

Ⓑ a favorite poem

Ⓒ an article in today's newspaper

Ⓓ a book on water safety

4. Which sentence does <u>not</u> use *quotation* correctly?

Ⓕ Alyssa included a quotation from the Bill of Rights in her talk.

Ⓖ When you write, you must place a quotation in quotation marks.

Ⓗ Mr. Keats starts each class with a quotation from his favorite book of poems.

Ⓙ A good reporter must always correctly quotation a source.

Writing   Imagine interviewing a famous person who does not speak the same language as you do. Write about that imagined experience. Be sure to use at least two of this week's words in your writing.

_____

_____

_____

_____

interpret • interpretation
clarify

Use the reproducible definitions on page 166 and the suggestions on page 6 to introduce the words for each day.

DAY 1

interpret
(verb) To explain the meaning of something. *Our teacher helped us* **interpret** *the poem.*

Say: *Sometimes written or spoken words may be hard to understand because they are complicated, use difficult words, or use images that are unclear. When this happens, we need to* **interpret** *the meaning, or explain it, in a way that is understandable.* Help students **interpret** a short poem, such as "Dreams" by Langston Hughes. Then have students complete the Day 1 activities on page 35. You may want to do the first one as a group.

DAY 2

interpretation
(noun) An explanation of the meaning of something. *Dr. Zee's* **interpretation** *of the test results surprised the other doctors.*

Say: *Not only words are interpreted. For example, a detective may have an* **interpretation** *of the evidence, or a scientist might have an* **interpretation** *of the results of an experiment.* Discuss what a detective or a scientist must do to develop an **interpretation** of the information they gather. (e.g., they must try to think of explanations for what they observe that agree with all the evidence or results) Then have students complete the Day 2 activities on page 35. You may want to do the first one as a group.

DAY 3

interpret
(verb) To orally translate from one language to another. *Yuri will* **interpret** *for his Russian-speaking father.*

Tell students that **interpret** and "translate" can be synonyms. Explain that **interpret** is used more often when referring to an immediate spoken—not written—translation from one language to another. Invite second-language learners or those who have traveled to a non-English-speaking country to demonstrate how to **interpret**. Then have students complete the Day 3 activities on page 36. You may want to do the first one as a group.

DAY 4

clarify
(verb) To make something clear. *The diagram will* **clarify** *how to assemble the bookshelf.*

Say: *When I don't understand something, I look for a way to* **clarify** *it, or make it easier to understand. For example, if a friend told me how to get to his home and I didn't understand, I might ask for a map to* **clarify** *the directions. When you ask me to explain the directions for an assignment again, you are asking me to* **clarify** *the instructions.* Ask students for examples of instances when they needed someone to **clarify** something. Then have students complete the Day 4 activities on page 36. You may want to do the first one as a group.

DAY 5

Have students complete page 37. Call on students to read aloud their answers to the writing activity.

Daily Academic Vocabulary

Day 1 interpret

1. How would you complete this sentence? Say it aloud to a partner.

Some poems are difficult to interpret because _____.

2. Which word means the same thing as *interpret?* Circle your answer.

a. repeat
b. explain
c. include
d. create

3. Which sentence uses *interpret* correctly? Circle your answer.

a. It is not polite to interpret.
b. I did not understand the story, so I asked my teacher to interpret it for me.
c. An interpret appeared in last Sunday's newspaper.
d. Could you interpret the passage so that I will not understand it?

Day 2 interpretation

1. How would you complete this sentence? Say it aloud to a partner.

My interpretation of the saying "Don't count your chickens before
they hatch" is _____.

2. Match each saying with a possible *interpretation.* Write its correct letter on the line.

___ "A friend in need is a friend indeed."

___ "Rome was not built in a day."

___ "The best things in life are free."

___ "Look before you leap."

a. Any big job takes time to do.

b. True friends help us in times of trouble.

c. Always think before you do something.

d. Money doesn't make us happy.

3. Which sentence does <u>not</u> use *interpretation* correctly? Circle your answer.

a. One student presented her interpretation of the story.
b. Everyone agrees with the lifeguard's interpretation of the pool rules.
c. My interpretation of the results is different from yours.
d. Officer Smith had to interpretation the information gathered at the scene.

Day 3 interpret

1. How would you complete this sentence? Say it aloud to a partner.

It must be difficult to interpret because _____.

2. Which sentence does <u>not</u> use *interpret* correctly? Circle your answer.

    a. I can interpret for the boy who speaks Spanish.

    b. Linda interprets for Gwen using American Sign Language.

    c. That kind of bird interprets a special song in the spring.

    d. I will study English so that I can interpret for my family.

3. Which phrase best completes this sentence? Circle your answer.

In order to interpret for our guest from Mexico, I would _____.

    a. have to know Spanish   c. buy a book in French

    b. talk very fast   d. watch a movie in Spanish

4. Give a specific example of a situation in which you would need someone to *interpret* for you.

_____

_____

Day 4 clarify

1. How would you complete this sentence? Say it aloud to a partner.

I once asked _____ to clarify _____.

2. Which of these might someone do if asked to *clarify* a statement he made? Circle your answers.

    a. repeat the statement exactly

    b. express the idea using different words

    c. ignore the request and continue talking

    d. add details to better explain what he said

3. Which sentences use *clarify* correctly? Circle your answers.

    a. We need to clarify the windows so we can see out better.

    b. The labels will clarify the space for the flower.

    c. Will you clarify the rules of the game for me?

    d. Ramon chose his words carefully when asked to clarify his idea.

Name_____

Daily
Academic
Vocabulary

Fill in the bubble next to the correct answer.

1. Which of these things might need to be *interpreted*?

Ⓐ a duck

Ⓑ a pot of stew

Ⓒ a poem

Ⓓ a forest

2. Which of these words means the same thing as *interpretation*?

Ⓕ importance

Ⓖ explanation

Ⓗ entertainment

Ⓙ happiness

3. Which sentence uses *interpret* correctly?

Ⓐ My sister interprets swimmers at college.

Ⓑ The kitchen interprets between the dining room and the living room.

Ⓒ Nancy interpreted the conversation for the visitor from China.

Ⓓ A cat will interpret a mouse under the table.

4. Which sentence does <u>not</u> use *clarify* correctly?

Ⓕ The tutor will clarify the assignment for the student.

Ⓖ Our teacher will discuss the poem to clarify it for us.

Ⓗ The principal asked the students to clarify their desks for the summer.

Ⓙ This diagram should clarify the rules of the game for you.

Writing   Using at least one of this week's words, write about a time when someone did not correctly *interpret* your facial expressions or your tone of voice.

_____

_____

_____

_____

estimate • estimation calculate

Use the reproducible definitions on page 167 and the suggestions on page 6 to introduce the words for each day.

DAY 1

estimate
(verb) To make a careful guess about something. *I **estimate** that it will take an hour to complete my work.*

Look at the class and say: *I **estimate** that (number) of you will watch TV tonight. I don't know for sure how many of you will, but I can guess.* Ask: *How many of your peers do you **estimate** will watch TV tonight?* Have students **estimate** other activities their peers will do this evening using the sentence starter, "I **estimate** that ___." Then have students complete the Day 1 activities on page 39. You may want to do the first one as a group.

DAY 2

estimate
(noun) A careful guess about the amount, size, cost, or value of something. *My **estimate** is that we will need three students for this project.*

Point out that while the noun and verb forms of **estimate** are spelled the same, there are differences in their pronunciations. (**estimate** as a verb: es´ tuh māt´; **estimate** as a noun: es´ tuh mit) Say: *Yesterday I made an **estimate** as to how many of you would watch TV last night.* Ask: *In what other situations do we use **estimates**? Why do we use **estimates**?* Then have students complete the Day 2 activities on page 39. You may want to do the first one as a group.

DAY 3

estimation
(noun) An opinion; judgment. *In my **estimation**, nothing is better to eat than ice cream.*

Say: *When we use the noun **estimation**, we are usually talking about making a judgment on quality.* Give statements such as, *In my **estimation**, green is the best color.* Then ask students to give their own statements, using, "In my **estimation**, ___." Then have students complete the Day 3 activities on page 40. You may want to do the first one as a group.

DAY 4

calculate
(verb) To find out an answer or result by using mathematics. *I can **calculate** the total cost of the trip based on the number of students who will be going.*

Tell students that this definition of **calculate** has to do with working with numbers. Say: *When we estimate using numbers, we might, for instance, round up the numbers to come up with a close, but not exact, answer. When we **calculate**, we compute an exact answer.* Say: *We can **calculate** the number of students in our school by adding the students in all the classes.* Then ask: *What do we call the instrument that helps us **calculate**?* (calculator) Have students complete the Day 4 activities on page 40. You may want to do the first one as a group.

DAY 5

Have students complete page 41. Call on students to read aloud their answers to the writing activity.

Name_____

Day 1 estimate

1. How would you complete this sentence? Say it aloud to a partner.

I estimate it will take me _____ to get home after school.

2. Which word means the same thing as the verb *estimate*? Circle your answer.

   a. know   c. guess

   b. research   d. wish

3. Which sentence shows someone *estimating*? Circle your answer.

   a. Rob knows the exact price is $37.42.

   b. Lily ran three miles around the track before she was tired.

   c. Sam needs the guest list for his birthday party.

   d. Rosa thinks she will need about two gallons of paint for her room.

4. *Estimate* how many students are in your school.

_____

Day 2 estimate

1. How would you complete this sentence? Say it aloud to a partner.

Someone might ask for an estimate on the cost or value of _____.

2. Which sentence uses the noun *estimate* correctly? Circle your answer.

   a. The salesperson gave us an estimate on the cost of a new computer.

   b. At the cash register, Mr. Rodriquez paid for the socks with the estimate.

   c. I gave the customer an exact estimate of the price.

   d. His estimate was to go away on vacation.

3. Give an *estimate* of the number of books you read in a year.

_____

4. How did you determine the *estimate* you gave for question 3?

_____

_____

Day 3 | estimation

1. How would you complete this sentence? Say it aloud to a partner.

In my estimation, the most important thing we do each day in school is _____.

2. Which of these best completes this sentence? Circle your answer.

In my estimation, _____.

    a. Zach thinks that we will have a test next week.

    b. I don't know what my opinion is about the situation.

    c. Mr. Olmos asked me to clean his windows.

    d. I think she is the best teacher I have ever had.

3. Which sentences use *estimation* correctly? Circle your answers.

    a. In the estimation of the judges, the Canadian skater did the best.

    b. The doctor's estimation was that I would need to stay in bed for two weeks.

    c. What is the planned estimation of your trip?

    d. I enjoyed the estimation last weekend.

Day 4 | calculate

1. How would you complete this sentence? Say it aloud to a partner.

Knowing how to calculate a sum without a calculator is important because _____.

2. In which of these situations did somebody *calculate* a result? Circle your answers.

    a. Jim guessed that the cost of his vacation will be within his budget.

    b. The customer added together the cost of each item to arrive at the total.

    c. Lenny wondered how long the trip to the city would take on the train.

    d. The carpenter found the area of the room by multiplying its length by its width.

3. Which of the following would you need to *calculate*? Circle your answers.

    a. the time of day

    b. how much time there is between now and when school ends

    c. the difference in ages between you and your favorite cousin

    d. your current age

Daily Academic Vocabulary

Day 5 estimate • estimation • calculate

Fill in the bubble next to the correct answer.

1. Which sentence does <u>not</u> use the verb *estimate* correctly?

Ⓐ I estimate that my final grade for the semester will be a "B."

Ⓑ I like to estimate hot dogs and hamburgers for lunch.

Ⓒ Kayla estimated the cost of the candy before she went to buy it.

Ⓓ He estimated that it would take two quarts of water to fill the fishbowl.

2. Which sentence uses the noun *estimate* correctly?

Ⓕ Can you provide an estimate of how long it will take to finish?

Ⓖ My estimate is that I have two eyes, one nose, and two ears.

Ⓗ I was delighted to receive an estimate for my birthday.

Ⓙ The billionaire's estimate was surrounded by a high wall.

I **estimate** that I have about 4,000 feathers!

3. Which of these is the best ending for this sentence?

In my estimation, _____.

Ⓐ my mother eats cereal for breakfast

Ⓑ December is the last month of the year

Ⓒ that is the best story that we've read this year

Ⓓ the bus takes us to school

4. Which sentence does <u>not</u> use *calculate* correctly?

Ⓕ Jasmine used her math skills to calculate the area of the room.

Ⓖ I divided the total into three parts to calculate the answer.

Ⓗ Olivia calculated the total cost by adding up how much she spent on each item.

Ⓙ Wilma will calculate at the piano for the recital.

Writing   You are at the store and have only a certain amount of money to spend. Will you be more likely to *calculate* or to *estimate* the cost of each item you need? Explain your answer using two of this week's words.

_____

_____

_____

CUMULATIVE REVIEW
WORDS FROM WEEKS 1–8

accomplish
accomplishment
assume
assumption
calculate
clarify
contend
convince
estimate
estimation
implication
imply
interpret
interpretation
perform
performance
persuade
persuasion
persuasive
presume
quotation
quote
standard
suppose
translate
translation
typical

Days 1–4

Each day's activity is a cloze paragraph that students complete with words or forms of words that they have learned in weeks 1–8. Before students begin, pronounce each word in the box on the student page, have students repeat each word, and then review each word's meaning(s). **Other ways to review the words:**

- Start a sentence containing one of the words and have students finish the sentence orally. For example:

  *One **assumption** younger students have about my grade is…*
  *The **implications** of not getting enough sleep are…*

- Provide students with a definition and ask them to supply the word that fits it.

- Ask questions that require students to know the meaning of each word. For example:

  *How many days do you **estimate** are left in the school year?*
  *Who would you expect to find **quoted** in the newspaper?*

- Have students use each word in a sentence.

Day 5

Start by reviewing the seven words not practiced on Days 1–4: **assumption, clarify, estimate, implication, persuasion, quote, suppose**. Write the words on the board and have students repeat them after you. Provide a sentence for one of the words. Ask students to think of their own sentence and share it with a partner. Call on several students to share their sentences. Follow the same procedure with the remaining words. Then have students complete the code-breaker activity.

Extension Ideas

Use any of the following activities to help integrate the vocabulary words into other content areas:

- Have students use **standard** units of measurement to follow a recipe and make a snack. Have students **calculate** the amount of each ingredient they will need to make enough for the entire class.

- Have students write **persuasive** letters to the school principal or local newspaper. Talk with students about the elements of **persuasion** and how those can be used in their letters.

- Have students find a famous **quotation** they like. Ask them to **interpret** the **quotation** in their own words.

 Daily Academic Vocabulary • EMC 2761 • © Evan-Moor Corporation

Name _____

| accomplishment | interpretation | perform | presumed | translation |
| contended | interpreted | persuaded | translated | typical |

Day 1

Fill in the blanks with words from the word box.

We watched a great film in science. It shows a _____ year in

the life of emperor penguins in Antarctica. It was originally filmed in French but was

_____ into English. The movie explained how males and females

work together to raise their chicks. Many of my classmates _____

the teamwork to mean that family is important, even to penguins. There are many

jobs penguin parents have to _____. The father cares for the egg

while the mother walks up to a hundred miles to the sea and back to gather food.

When a chick hatches, it is quite an _____!

Day 2

Fill in the blanks with words from the word box.

I never knew much about ballet, so I always _____ that

it was boring. My sister _____ that it is much better than TV.

She often tried to convince me to go to the ballet. The other night, I was finally

_____. We went to a ballet called "Swan Lake." It was based on

an old German legend. There was no need for a _____ into English

because the story was told through movement. The dancers explained the story of

a princess who was turned into a swan. Their _____ of the story

was beautiful. Now I am a fan!

| accomplished | calculate | estimation | performances | quotation |
| assume | convinced | implied | persuasive | standard |

Day 3

Fill in the blanks with words from the word box.

I read a _____ that said "Superman can fly faster than the

speed of light." Why doesn't he "fly faster than the speed of sound"? If, in your

_____, the answer is because light travels faster than sound, you

are correct! Think of a thunderstorm. In a _____ storm, you see

lightning before hearing thunder. The light from lightning reaches your eyes before

the sound of thunder reaches your ears. You can count the difference in time to

_____ how far away the storm is. For every five seconds between

lightning and thunder, you can _____ you are about one mile away

from the storm.

Day 4

Fill in the blanks with words from the word box.

The silence of the crowd _____ the importance of the skateboarding

contest. Besides a cash prize, the winner would get her picture on the cover of a magazine.

A team of judges scored the skaters' _____. Kyla was the last to go. Her

coach was _____ that a new trick would help her win. Kyla was doubtful,

but her coach was _____. She decided to follow his plan. She took off

down the ramp, flipped into the air, and landed successfully! She _____

the trick and won the contest!

Name _____

Daily Academic Vocabulary

Day 5

Crack the Code!

Write one of the words from the word box on the lines next to each clue.

accomplish	contend	interpret	persuasive	translate
accomplishment	convince	interpretation	presume	translation
assume	estimate	perform	quotation	typical
assumption	estimation	performance	quote	
calculate	implication	persuade	standard	
clarify	imply	persuasion	suppose	

1. to repeat words that were spoken or written by someone else __ __ __ __ __

1

2. to make a careful guess about something __ __ __ __ __ __ __ __

2

3. something suggested, but not said __ __ __ __ __ __ __ __ __ __ __

3   4

4. something that is supposed __ __ __ __ __ __ __ __ __ __

5   6

5. the act of convincing someone __ __ __ __ __ __ __ __ __ __

7

6. to believe or think __ __ __ __ __ __ __

8

7. to make clear or easier to understand __ __ __ __ __ __ __

9

Now use the numbers under the letters to crack the code. Write the letters on the lines below. The words will answer this question:

Which penguin is the largest penguin?

__ h __   __ __ __ __ __ __ __   __ __ __ g __ __ __

1   2   2 3 6 2 7 8 7   6 2 4   5 9 4

refer • reference

Use the reproducible definitions on page 168 and the suggestions on page 6 to introduce the words for each day.

DAY 1

refer
(verb) To speak of, mention, or call attention to someone or something. *Books often **refer** to famous events in history.*

Tell students that when we **refer** to something, we are usually not going to go into detail about it. We might **refer** to it because it is related to what we are talking about. Say: *A book about the American bald eagle might **refer** to another bird to help us understand something about the eagle.* Invite students to suggest other examples. (e.g., you might **refer** to a character from a book who reminds you of a friend) Then have students complete the Day 1 activities on page 47. You may want to do the first one as a group.

DAY 2

reference
(noun) A mention of someone or something. *There was a **reference** to our school in the newspaper yesterday.*

Say: *When we refer to something, we make a **reference** to it.* Write "**reference**" on the board and underline the base word "refer." Say: *For example, a book about the American bald eagle might make a **reference** to another large bird, perhaps the red-tailed hawk.* Show examples of **references** from student textbooks or newspaper articles. Then have students complete the Day 2 activities on page 47. You may want to do the first one as a group.

DAY 3

refer
(verb) To turn to for help or information. ***Refer** to the encyclopedia for facts about the country of Brazil.*

Say: *We use **refer** in this way when we are talking about finding information, an answer, or some other kind of help. You might **refer** to an expert in the form of a person or a book.* Ask: *If you have a question about how to play your new computer game, to what expert might you **refer**?* Then say: ***Refer** can also be used to tell you to turn to or look at something. Sometimes a textbook will tell you to **refer** to an illustration or a figure.* Show examples from textbooks. Then have students complete the Day 3 activities on page 48. You may want to do the first one as a group.

DAY 4

reference
(noun) A source of information. *My grammar handbook is a good **reference** for the rules of punctuation.*

Ask: *What **references** might you find in the classroom or library?* Say: *People can be **references**, too. When someone applies for a job, he or she may be asked for a **reference**. The **reference** is someone who knows the person and can tell the new employer information about that person.* Then have students complete the Day 4 activities on page 48. You may want to do the first one as a group.

DAY 5

Have students complete page 49. Call on students to read aloud their answers to the writing activity.

Name_____

Day 1 refer

1. How would you complete this sentence? Say it aloud to a partner.

If I received an award, I would refer to _____ in my "thank-you" speech.

2. Which sentence uses *refer* correctly? Circle your answer.

    a. Aunt Jane often refers to her days as a cheerleader.

    b. The refer in the last paragraph of the essay confused me.

    c. You should never refer in anger until you have had a chance to calm down.

    d. I like to refer to the living room after dinner.

3. Who is most likely to *refer* to today's football game in his or her newspaper article? Circle your answer.

    a. the movie critic   c. the cartoonist

    b. the sportswriter   d. the editor

Day 2 reference

1. How would you complete this sentence? Say it aloud to a partner.

If someone on television made a reference to one of my friends, I would _____.

2. If I wrote an essay about myself, I would make a *reference* to the following three people who have influenced me:

    a. _____

    b. _____

    c. _____

3. Which sentence does <u>not</u> use *reference* correctly? Circle your answer.

    a. This article makes a reference to my brother's team.

    b. In her speech, the mayor made a reference to the new park.

    c. I was confused by the reference to a writer I don't know.

    d. My parents are making a reference at the bank.

Day 3 | refer

1. How would you complete this sentence? Say it aloud to a partner.

I would refer to my teacher if _____.

2. Which sentence does not use *refer* correctly? Circle your answer.

a. Refer to the dictionary for the correct spelling of that word.

b. I had to refer to the directions in order to play the game.

c. You must refer often to make this easy to read.

d. I'll refer to my class notes to remind myself about the important ideas.

3. Which phrase could complete this sentence? Circle your answer.

If you have a question about the history of our town, refer to _____.

a. the town historian   c. the dictionary

b. the phone book   d. *Goodnight Moon*

Day 4 | reference

1. How would you complete this sentence? Say it aloud to a partner.

The best reference for answering a science question is _____.

2. Name three *references* you often use in your schoolwork.

a. _____

b. _____

c. _____

3. Which of these books would not be a good *reference* for a report on Russia? Circle your answer.

a. *Russia: Its Land and People*

b. *A History of the American People*

c. *World Book Encyclopedia*

d. *The World Almanac*

What is a good **reference** for information on space exploration?

Name_____

Day 5 refer • reference

Fill in the bubble next to the correct answer.

1. Which sentence uses *refer* correctly?

Ⓐ My relatives often refer to my great-grandfather when they talk about family history.

Ⓑ A refer is an important thing to have at school.

Ⓒ I refer the mistake I made on the test.

Ⓓ We refer our teacher because he is so nice.

2. In which book is a *reference* to a favorite food most likely to appear?

Ⓕ *The History of Middle Earth*

Ⓖ *Great Inventions*

Ⓗ *The Joy of Cooking*

Ⓙ *How to Play the Piano*

3. Which source would you *refer* to for information about cleaning your fish tank?

Ⓐ a gardener

Ⓑ *Merriam-Webster's Dictionary*

Ⓒ a book on keeping fish as pets

Ⓓ a book on great places to go fishing

4. Which *reference* would you expect your doctor to use?

Ⓕ a medical encyclopedia

Ⓖ a book with summaries of movies

Ⓗ a collection of stories

Ⓙ a biography about a famous athlete

Writing   Describe a time when you used the library to do research on a topic.
Use this week's words in your writing.

_____

_____

_____

_____

WEEK 11

specify • specific
detail • in detail

Use the reproducible definitions on page 169 and the suggestions on page 6 to introduce the words for each day.

DAY 1

specify
(verb) To name or say something exactly. *Mr. Winter will **specify** which problems we have to do for homework.*

specific
(adj.) Particular, definite, or individually named. *Please show me the **specific** book that you want to read.*

Say: *When you **specify** something, you have picked it out from other things in a group. When we **specify** one thing, we are being **specific**. If someone asked me to **specify** my favorite flavor of ice cream, I would say that the **specific** flavor I like is (chocolate).* Ask students to **specify** their favorite foods or books. Have them respond by saying, "The **specific** flavor I like most is ___." Then say: *You might be asked to "be **specific**" when you give answers in your schoolwork. For instance, if I asked you to be **specific** about why you think a book is good or not, what would you do?* (Give examples that illustrate your opinion.) Then have students complete the Day 1 activities on page 51. You may want to do the first one as a group.

DAY 2

detail
(noun) A small part of a whole thing. *I missed that **detail** about the party because I read the invitation too quickly.*

Say: ***Details** are the small things that are part of a larger whole. Sometimes **details** are not important, but many times they are.* Ask students to talk about their favorite place in general. Then ask them to mention a **detail** about that place. Then have students complete the Day 2 activities on page 51. You may want to do the first one as a group.

DAY 3

detail
(verb) To describe or tell very precisely. *I will **detail** each step in the process so that you will know exactly what to do.*

Say: *When you **detail** something, you are very precise, or exact, in your description. For example, I might ask you to **detail** how you arrived at an answer to a math problem.* Ask students for examples of other situations in which they might be asked to **detail** something. Then have students complete the Day 3 activities on page 52. You may want to do the first one as a group.

DAY 4

in detail
(adv. phrase) Thoroughly, with attention to specifics. *William described **in detail** everything he had done on his vacation.*

Say: *If I asked you to describe **in detail** what you did during the lunch period, I would want you to include many facts about what you did. What could you say?* After a student responds, ask: *Did he or she tell **in detail** about the lunch period? Why or why not?* Then ask: *What are some specific times when you might tell about something **in detail**?* Then have students complete the Day 4 activities on page 52. You may want to do the first one as a group.

DAY 5

Have students complete page 53. Call on students to read aloud their answers to the writing activity.

Name_____

Day 1 · specify • specific

1. How would you complete these sentences? Say them aloud to a partner.

If someone asked me to specify my favorite food, I would say _____.

The specific after-school activity I like the best is _____.

2. In which sentences is *specify* used correctly? Circle your answers.

a. Please specify the kind of bicycle you would like to own.

b. In specify, I would vote for Conrad for president.

c. The bicycle specifies the best way to go up the hill.

d. Uncle Henry specified the kind of dessert he wanted.

3. List two *specific* goals you have for yourself this year.

a. _____

b. _____

4. In which of these sentences is someone being *specific*? Circle your answer.

a. "I think that's a nice painting."

b. "That painting looks good."

c. "I like the vivid colors in that painting."

d. "I saw that painting in an art book."

Day 2 · detail

1. How would you complete this sentence? Say it aloud to a partner.

One detail I would like to change about school would be _____.

2. List three *details* from a story you just read.

a. _____

b. _____

c. _____

3. Which of the following is a *detail* on a bicycle? Circle your answer.

a. the wheels

b. the handlebars

c. the color of the bell

d. the pedals

Day 3 **detail**

1. How would you complete this sentence? Say it aloud to a partner.

I saw a show on television that detailed _____.

2. Which sentences use *detail* correctly? Circle your answers.

   a. I detailed the test.

   b. The instructions detailed what we had to do for the project.

   c. The waiter detailed the tea and coffee.

   d. The guidebook details the trail and what you will see while hiking it.

3. You are *detailing* the steps you take to prepare for a math test. Which of these would most likely <u>not</u> be on your list? Circle your answer.

   a. reread the chapter in my math book

   b. look over my math papers and correct errors

   c. count the number of times I have taken math tests

   d. practice solving math problems

4. *Detail* the process you follow when checking out a library book.

_____

_____

Day 4 **in detail**

1. How would you complete this sentence? Say it aloud to a partner.

I could tell you in detail how to _____.

2. Which sentence tells about the beginning of Erin's day *in detail*? Circle your answer.

   a. She got out of bed.

   b. She woke up at 7:04 a.m., yawned, stretched, and threw off the covers.

   c. She got out of bed like she always does.

   d. She got up and went to school.

3. Who is most likely to be able to explain *in detail* how to fly the space shuttle? Circle your answer.

   a. a science teacher   c. the mayor

   b. an astronaut   d. a race car driver

Name_____

Day 5 specify • specific • detail • in detail

Fill in the bubble next to the correct answer.

1. Which sentence uses *specify* correctly?

Ⓐ Please specify which of the menu items you would like to have for lunch.

Ⓑ Please specify your answer by choosing all the possible answers.

Ⓒ Specify, Maya went to the party after all.

Ⓓ Roast beef is the specify of the restaurant.

2. In which sentence is the speaker being *specific* about her plans for lunch?

Ⓕ I am hungry.

Ⓖ I would like to eat lunch soon.

Ⓗ I will have a turkey sandwich for lunch at Rosie's Place.

Ⓙ I had a sandwich there yesterday.

3. Which of the following is <u>not</u> a *detail* about a car?

Ⓐ It was made in the year 2004.

Ⓑ Its color is light brown.

Ⓒ It has been driven almost 50,000 miles.

Ⓓ It looks like a regular car.

Be **specific** when you tell me what you love about me.

4. Which sentence uses *detail* correctly?

Ⓕ I could detail in the game tomorrow.

Ⓖ The plumber detailed how to fix the leak.

Ⓗ I detailed when I slept last night.

Ⓙ My brother details the television every night.

Writing   Describe the furnishings of your room *in detail*. Be sure to name *specific* items of furniture and *specify* the colors in the room. Use at least two of this week's words in your description.

_____

_____

_____

_____

complicate • complicated
complication • complex

Use the reproducible definitions on page 170 and the suggestions on page 6 to introduce the words for each day.

DAY 1

complicate
(verb) To make something more difficult to do or understand. *If you forget to bring your lunch, it will complicate our day.*

complicated
(adj.) Hard to understand or difficult to do. *All of the questions on the test are too complicated to answer.*

Say: *When something makes it harder to do something else, it can be said to "complicate matters." If, for instance, you forget to bring your books to school, how would that complicate your day?* If students have trouble getting started, suggest that forgetting your books would mean borrowing or sharing books. Then ask: *What are other ways in which a school day can be complicated?* Encourage students to use the words **complicate** or **complicated** in their responses. Then have students complete the Day 1 activities on page 55. You may want to do the first one as a group.

DAY 2

complication
(noun) A difficulty that causes a problem. *When her car broke down, finding another way to get to work was a complication for my mother.*

Say: *Sometimes when we think a task will be simple, a complication, or difficulty, arises. For example, you may plan to bicycle to school in the morning, but then you notice that your bike has a flat. The flat tire is a complication that makes your plan to bicycle to school harder to do.* Ask students to describe a **complication** that they have experienced. Then have students complete the Day 2 activities on page 55. You may want to do the first one as a group.

DAY 3

complex
(adj.) Made up of many parts. *Automobiles are complex machines.*

Tell students that most of our electronic equipment is **complex**, having many small but important parts. Say: *Other things and situations in life can be complex, too. For instance, planning a science project can be a complex process. You must make many decisions about what you want to do and how you will do it.* Ask students to give examples of events that would be **complex** to plan. (e.g., a flight to the moon; a very large party) Then have students complete the Day 3 activities on page 56. You may want to do the first one as a group.

DAY 4

complex
(adj.) Very difficult to understand or do. *This game is too complex for younger kids.*

Say: *Problems or situations with many parts can be complex, or hard to understand.* Ask students for examples of **complex** problems or situations they have faced. Then have students complete the Day 4 activities on page 56. You may want to do the first one as a group.

DAY 5

Have students complete page 57. Call on students to read aloud their answers to the writing activity.

Name_____

Day 1 complicate • complicated

1. How would you complete these sentences? Say them aloud to a partner.

It complicates my day when _____.

I think that _____ is the most complicated subject to learn.

2. Which sentence uses *complicate* correctly? Circle your answer.

    a. She didn't want to complicate matters by bringing her dog.

    b. Sometimes I complicate on the weekends.

    c. I like to complicate in as many sports as I can.

    d. The electrical complicate matter confused the electrician.

3. Which of the following is a *complicated* task? Circle your answer.

    a. sharpening your pencil

    b. putting on your coat

    c. writing your name on a piece of paper

    d. building a model of your school

4. What would you do if you found *complicated* directions on a test?

_____

_____

Day 2 complication

1. How would you complete this sentence? Say it aloud to a partner.

I experienced a complication when _____.

2. Which of the following is an example of an unexpected *complication* a gardener might face? Circle your answer.

    a. seeds that need to be planted

    b. plants that need to be watered

    c. ripe vegetables that need to be picked

    d. a snowstorm in the spring

3. Which of the following means the same thing as *complication*? Circle your answer.

    a. difficulty   c. delight

    b. entertainment   d. solution

What **complications** could arise while riding a bicycle?

Day 3 complex

1. How would you complete this sentence? Say it aloud to a partner.

I think the most complex piece of equipment at our school is _____.

2. Which of the following things is *complex*? Circle your answer.

   a. a basketball   c. a hammer
   b. a DVD player   d. a rock

3. Which sentence does <u>not</u> use the word *complex* correctly? Circle your answer.

   a. Please do not complex the problem.
   b. The committee presented a complex plan for school improvement.
   c. The jeweler took apart the complex watch.
   d. I built a complex model of the space shuttle.

Day 4 complex

1. How would you complete this sentence? Say it aloud to a partner.

An idea I find complex is _____.

2. Which sentence uses the word *complex* correctly? Circle your answer.

   a. Because of the complex instructions, it was easy to build the toy.
   b. It was a complex problem that took much thought to solve.
   c. Kristen and Joe were able to complex the party by arriving late.
   d. I described the problem in complex.

3. Which of these tasks is the most *complex*? Circle your answer.

   a. sweeping the floor
   b. drying the dishes
   c. building a computer
   d. washing the windows

4. Explain something you know how to do that is *complex*.

_____

_____

Name_____

Daily
Academic
Vocabulary

Fill in the bubble next to the correct answer.

1. Which sentence does <u>not</u> use *complicate* correctly?

Ⓐ The late arrival of the bus complicated my day.

Ⓑ This unexpected storm complicates our plans.

Ⓒ Do not complicate matters by asking unnecessary questions.

Ⓓ The complicate on the exam confused me.

2. Which sentence describes a *complex* object?

Ⓕ This toothbrush has a handle and plastic bristles.

Ⓖ This computer includes software, electronics, a keyboard, and a mouse.

Ⓗ This cereal bowl is round and blue.

Ⓙ This sock is red and is made from cotton.

3. Which sentence uses *complication* correctly?

Ⓐ The highway repair work is a complication for drivers.

Ⓑ A complication is a welcome event.

Ⓒ I am reading a complication of stories.

Ⓓ That game is too complication to play.

4. Which phrase best completes this sentence?

This _____ is too complex for the average person to understand.

Ⓕ comic strip in the newspaper

Ⓖ book about Winnie the Pooh

Ⓗ article about heart attacks written for doctors

Ⓙ puzzle on the back of the cereal box

Writing Describe a situation that *complicated* your life at one time.
Use at least one of this week's words in your description.

_____

_____

_____

_____

defend • viewpoint
position • perspective

Use the reproducible definitions on page 171 and the suggestions on page 6 to introduce the words for each day.

DAY 1

defend
(verb) To argue or speak in support of something. *The school board members* **defend** *their decision to make the school day longer.*

Say: *When we present our side in an argument or discussion, we* **defend** *our ideas or opinions. When we* **defend** *what we think or believe, we use facts to support our opinion.* Ask: *Describe a time that you needed to* **defend** *your opinion on something. How did you* **defend** *it?* Then have students complete the Day 1 activities on page 59. You may want to do the first one as a group.

DAY 2

viewpoint
(noun) An opinion or way of thinking about something. *My friend and I share a common* **viewpoint** *on many subjects.*

Say: *We use the term* **viewpoint** *most often to talk about how we understand things based on what we know or believe to be true.* Ask: *What are some areas in which your* **viewpoint** *is different from your parents'? Why do you think your* **viewpoints** *are different?* Then have students complete the Day 2 activities on page 59. You may want to do the first one as a group.

DAY 3

position
(noun) A person's opinion or point of view on an issue or subject. *I took the* **position** *that we should recycle paper in our classroom.*

Point out that **position** has a similar meaning to the previous day's word. Say: *Both* **position** *and "viewpoint" refer to your opinion or where you stand on an issue.* Ask: *What is your* **position** *on sports? Homework?* Encourage students to use the word **position** in their statements. Then have students complete the Day 3 activities on page 60. You may want to do the first one as a group.

DAY 4

perspective
(noun) A particular view or way of looking at something. *From my mom's* **perspective***, my music is too loud.*

Say: ***Perspective***, like "position" and "viewpoint," is a particular way of looking at or thinking about something. For example, from my* **perspective** *as a teacher, students should read more than they watch TV. How might your* **perspective** *agree or disagree with mine? Why would your* **perspective** *differ?* (e.g., have different viewpoints; have different positions on the issue) Make sure students use vocabulary words from this week in their explanations. Then have students complete the Day 4 activities on page 60. You may want to do the first one as a group.

DAY 5

Have students complete page 61. Call on students to read aloud their answers to the writing activity.

**Daily
Academic
Vocabulary**

Day 1 defend

1. How would you complete this sentence? Say it aloud to a partner.

I could defend my opinion that _____.

2. Which sentence does not use *defend* correctly? Circle your answer.

a. The senator was able to defend his point of view on new taxes.
b. The student council had to defend its opinion on school uniforms.
c. Our teacher will defend on us to complete homework assignments.
d. Be prepared to defend your beliefs with strong arguments.

3. List three reasons you would present to *defend* the opinion that recess should be longer.

a. _____

b. _____

c. _____

4. How would you *defend* your best friend if someone said he or she was mean?

_____

_____

Day 2 viewpoint

1. How would you complete this sentence? Say it aloud to a partner.

My friend and I have different viewpoints on the topic of _____.

2. Who is most likely to have the *viewpoint* that we need more missions to outer space? Circle your answer.

a. a sailor   c. an astronaut
b. a mountain climber   d. a deep-sea diver

3. Which phrase does not mean about the same thing as the underlined phrase? Circle your answer.

From your viewpoint, what are the three best winter activities?

a. In your opinion   c. From your point of view
b. In conclusion   d. Based on your experiences

Name_____

Day 3 position

1. How would you complete this sentence? Say it aloud to a partner.

My position on the need for a longer school year is that _____.

2. Which sentence uses the word *position* correctly? Circle your answer.

a. I position on the idea of banning candy bars in school.

b. The mayor must defend her position on this issue.

c. That green plant has a position on the three leaves.

d. Will you position with me when I write the paper?

3. Which of these things would you do before taking a *position* on an important issue? Circle your answer.

a. learn as much about the issue as possible

b. go out to a restaurant

c. write an angry letter to the newspaper

d. watch your favorite television show

4. Describe your *position* on longer school days.

_____

_____

Day 4 perspective

1. How would you complete this sentence? Say it aloud to a partner.

From my perspective, _____ is the most fun thing to do on weekends.

2. Who is most likely to see the world from a *perspective* similar to yours? Circle your answer.

a. a famous athlete   c. the president of France

b. your best friend   d. a child in preschool

3. Which sentence does <u>not</u> use *perspective* correctly? Circle your answer.

a. From the scientists' perspective, the fossils were an important discovery.

b. My great-aunt's perspective on greeting cards is that people should make their own.

c. I perspective that we should grow more vegetables in the garden.

d. From the perspective of a person in a wheelchair, the curbs are too high.

Day 5 **defend • viewpoint • position • perspective**

Fill in the bubble next to the correct answer.

1. Which statement is not an example of someone *defending* an opinion?

Ⓐ "I don't deserve a ticket for speeding because my speedometer is broken."

Ⓑ "I think we should study spelling because it is a basic skill that everyone needs."

Ⓒ "He should not be punished for missing the test because he was sick."

Ⓓ "The United States of America has an elected president, not a king or queen."

2. What is the *viewpoint* that a school principal is most likely to have?

Ⓕ The school should close if it is raining outside.

Ⓖ Students should be on time for school every day.

Ⓗ Students should never have to take tests.

Ⓙ The students should make all the decisions about the school.

3. Which sentence uses *position* correctly?

Ⓐ I position that we should have the picnic in the park.

Ⓑ It is my position that a picnic is not complete without potato salad.

Ⓒ The ants have a position on the hot dog that I planned to eat.

Ⓓ The park ranger will not position us to build a campfire.

4. Which sentence uses *perspective* correctly?

Ⓕ Until I perspective, I cannot form an opinion.

Ⓖ From my perspective, the weekend is always too short.

Ⓗ The driver tried to perspective around the corner without looking.

Ⓙ Always perspective before you make an important decision.

Writing   What is your *viewpoint* on the amount of homework that you do each week? Use at least two of this week's words in your explanation.

_____

_____

_____

_____

assign • assignment
delegate • designate

Use the reproducible definitions on page 172 and the suggestions on page 6 to introduce the words for each day.

DAY 1

assign
(verb) To give as a task or duty. *Why do teachers **assign** homework that is due on Monday?*

assignment
(noun) A specific job or task that is given to somebody. *My dad's **assignment** was to clean out the garage.*

Say: *If I give you homework, I **assign** homework. If I tell a student to erase the board, I **assign** the task to that student. The homework and the erasing of the board are **assignments**.* Ask: *What have I **assigned** today? What **assignments** have you completed today?* Then ask students for examples of **assignments** (jobs or tasks) that someone outside of school might **assign** to them. Have students complete the Day 1 activities on page 63. You may want to do the first one as a group.

DAY 2

assign
(verb) To set apart or give out for a particular use. *The librarians **assign** these shelves for the books on music.*

Tell students that when we use the verb **assign** in this way, we are not talking about **assigning** people, but instead things or places. Say: *For example, a room in every home is **assigned** for cooking.* Ask: *What are some of the sections of the classroom or school building that have been **assigned** for specific uses?* Then have students complete the Day 2 activities on page 63. You may want to do the first one as a group.

DAY 3

delegate
(verb) To give someone else the responsibility to do something. *Our parents **delegate** the small chores to my sister and me.*

Say: *One of the things a person in charge does is to **delegate** tasks. He or she makes each task someone else's responsibility. Tasks are often **delegated** to you as part of a group project.* Ask: *What tasks have been **delegated** to you? When did that happen? Have you ever **delegated** tasks? When?* Then have students complete the Day 3 activities on page 64. You may want to do the first one as a group.

DAY 4

designate
(verb) To choose for a particular job or purpose. *Our teacher will **designate** someone to erase the board.*

Say: *When you delegate someone a task, you **designate** him or her for that task.* Ask a student to do a short task. Say: *I **designated** (student) to do that task. As a teacher, I often **designate** students for specific jobs.* Ask: *What jobs do I **designate** to you?* Then ask: *In sports, what jobs do coaches **designate**?* (e.g., team captains; positions) Say: *Places can also be **designated** for particular purposes.* Ask: *What kinds of places are **designated** as preserved or protected areas?* Have students complete the Day 4 activities on page 64. You may want to do the first one as a group.

DAY 5

Have students complete page 65. Call on students to read aloud their answers to the writing activity.

Name _____

Day 1 assign • assignment

1. How would you complete these sentences? Say them aloud to a partner.

I like to be assigned to _____.

The hardest assignment I've ever had was _____.

2. Which phrase best completes this sentence? Circle your answer.

Mr. Ayers assigned _____.

a. a good dinner   c. one page of math problems

b. my favorite television show   d. going on a trip

3. List three *assignments* that you received at school or at home last week.

a. _____

b. _____

c. _____

4. What chores are you *assigned* at home?

_____

_____

Day 2 assign

1. How would you complete this sentence? Say it aloud to a partner.

In my room at home, I have assigned a special place for _____.

2. Which sentence uses *assign* correctly? Circle your answer.

a. I assign my room every Saturday.

b. This corner of the garage is assigned to the lawnmower.

c. In the assign, we are asked to write a description of a lake.

d. It took only seconds to assign down that hill.

3. Which phrases best complete this sentence? Circle your answers.

When organizing the classroom, let's remember to assign an area for _____.

a. spelling words   c. your math paper

b. a reading corner   d. our computers

Name_____

Day 3 delegate

1. How would you complete this sentence? Say it aloud to a partner.

I wish I could delegate _____ to _____ for me.

2. Which sentences use *delegate* correctly? Circle your answers.

    a. Ms. Santoro delegated the job of collecting the papers to me.

    b. In delegating vegetables, it is important to choose fresh ones.

    c. The team delegated the game because of rain.

    d. That duty has been delegated to my assistant.

3. Who is most likely to have the power to *delegate* responsibilities in a club? Circle your answer.

    a. the newest member   c. the club president

    b. somebody who hopes to join the club   d. the club mascot

4. What jobs have been *delegated* to you in the past?

_____

_____

Day 4 designate

1. How would you complete this sentence? Say it aloud to a partner.

I hope the teacher designates me to _____.

2. Which sentences do <u>not</u> use *designate* correctly? Circle your answers.

    a. The president designates his or her vice president.

    b. To designate something, I must do it myself.

    c. The coach designated the game.

    d. Colin was designated to organize the closet.

3. Which type of person would you *designate* as a group leader? Circle your answer.

    a. someone who is funny and unorganized

    b. someone who knows nothing about the group

    c. someone who likes to have all of the attention

    d. someone who is fair, listens, and keeps everyone on track

You should **designate** me as your class mascot!

Day 5 assign • assignment • delegate • designate

Fill in the bubble next to the correct answer.

1. Which sentence uses the word *assign* correctly?

  Ⓐ A halo around the moon is assign of rain.

  Ⓑ Mr. Azzul assigned an essay on our favorite sport.

  Ⓒ I assign when I ride to school in the morning.

  Ⓓ Justin has assigned from the club.

2. Which of the following would <u>not</u> be a common *assignment* for students?

  Ⓕ to study vocabulary words

  Ⓖ to read a chapter of a book

  Ⓗ to wash the classroom windows

  Ⓙ to write a report

3. Which of these sentences does <u>not</u> use *assign* correctly?

  Ⓐ This shelf has been assigned for history books.

  Ⓑ I did not understand the assign.

  Ⓒ Some trails in the park are assigned only for bicycles.

  Ⓓ Please assign a part of your day to homework.

4. Which dinnertime task might be *delegated* to a younger sister or brother?

  Ⓕ cooking the meal

  Ⓖ sharpening a knife

  Ⓗ checking the oven temperature

  Ⓙ setting the table

Writing   What places in your town or community have been *designated* for
a special purpose, such as a historical landmark or nature preserve?
Be sure to use a form of the word *designate* in your writing.

_____

_____

_____

_____

WEEK 15

apply • application applicable

Use the reproducible definitions on page 173 and the suggestions on page 6 to introduce the words for each day.

DAY 1

apply
(verb) To put into action or use. *In this experiment, you will **apply** what you learned yesterday about liquids.*

Say: *We can **apply**, or use, things that are real objects. For example, we can **apply** the brakes on a bicycle. We can also use the word **apply** for things that we cannot see or touch, such as when we **apply** math skills to solving a problem.* Ask students to tell about a time when they **applied** math knowledge to solve a real-life problem. Then have students complete the Day 1 activities on page 67. You may want to do the first one as a group.

DAY 2

application
(noun) A way of being used. *Electricity has many **applications** in our lives.*

Hold up a sheet of paper. Ask: *What are some **applications** for, or ways of using, this sheet of paper?* Encourage students to "think outside the box," such as making a paper airplane or using it as a funnel. Then ask: *Can you think of objects in your everyday lives that have more than one **application**?* (e.g., rulers; pencils; sponges; towels) Then have students complete the Day 2 activities on page 67. You may want to do the first one as a group.

DAY 3

apply
(verb) To be suitable for; to have to do with something. *The rules of conduct **apply** to everyone in the classroom.*

Tell students that we use **apply** in this way when we mean that something suits or fits a situation. Say: *For instance, the rules of fair play **apply** to every sport. Those rules fit every sport. They are appropriate for every sport.* Ask: *What are rules that **apply** to you in school?* Then have students complete the Day 3 activities on page 68. You may want to do the first one as a group.

DAY 4

applicable
(adj.) Being well suited for something. *Your advice is **applicable** to many situations.*

Say: *When something—like a rule, for instance—applies, then we say that it is **applicable**.* Point out that some things are **applicable** in all situations, while other things are only **applicable** in special situations. Say: *For example, the rule about stopping at red lights is **applicable** to all traffic—cars, motorcycles, and bicycles. But the rule about always wearing a helmet is **applicable** only to bicycle and motorcycle riders, not drivers of cars.* Then have students complete the Day 4 activities on page 68. You may want to do the first one as a group.

DAY 5

Have students complete page 69. Call on students to read aloud their answers to the writing activity.

Day 1 apply

1. How would you complete this sentence? Say it aloud to a partner.

One example of how I apply my knowledge is when I _____.

2. Which sentence does not use apply correctly? Circle your answer.

a. I apply a comb to my hair to style it.
b. The bus driver applies the brakes when coming to a stop sign.
c. If you apply your skills and talents, you will accomplish great things.
d. I enjoy applying books in a bookstore.

3. List three strategies that you apply to learn the meaning of new words.

a. _____

b. _____

c. _____

Day 2 application

1. How would you complete this sentence? Say it aloud to a partner.

One tool or object that has many applications is _____.

2. Which sentences use application correctly? Circle your answers.

a. One application of a ruler is to use it as a straight edge for drawing lines.
b. The cleaner in the spray bottle has many applications.
c. The application up the mountain was not a success.
d. I application my best efforts.

3. Which of these tasks are not applications of a shovel? Circle your answers.

a. mowing a lawn
b. removing snow from a driveway
c. digging a hole
d. cutting tree branches

4. What is an application for a spoon? Be creative.

_____

_____

Name_____

Day 3 apply

1. How would you complete this sentence? Say it aloud to a partner.

A rule that applies to this classroom is _____.

2. Which statements *apply* to the public library? Circle your answers.

    a. It does not cost money to check out a book.

    b. Nobody is allowed to touch anything.

    c. You must stand in line for hours.

    d. If a book is not returned on time, a fine must be paid.

3. Write two statements that *apply* to your family.

    a. _____

    b. _____

4. How does academic vocabulary *apply* to school?

_____

_____

Day 4 applicable

1. How would you complete this sentence? Say it aloud to a partner.

An applicable reminder when going swimming would be _____.

2. Which statements are *applicable* to the lifeguards on a beach? Circle your answers.

    a. They work indoors.

    b. They watch for swimmers who are having problems in the water.

    c. They are afraid of the water.

    d. They know how to swim.

3. Which statement is <u>not</u> *applicable* to taking a test? Circle your answer.

    a. Read the directions carefully.

    b. Read all the questions carefully.

    c. Review all the answer choices before answering.

    d. Buckle your seat belt when riding in a car.

This outfit is probably not **applicable** to all situations.

Name_____

Day 5 **apply • application • applicable**

Fill in the bubble next to the correct answer.

1. Which sentence does <u>not</u> use *apply* correctly?

Ⓐ The rules must be applied the same way in all cases.

Ⓑ Trina applied what she learned yesterday in her skating lesson today.

Ⓒ You must apply force to open this door.

Ⓓ Jorge applies every day after he does his homework.

2. Which of these would <u>not</u> be an *application* of fire while on a camping trip?

Ⓕ using it to stay warm

Ⓖ using it to toast marshmallows

Ⓗ using it to see at night

Ⓙ using it to fish

3. Which sentence uses *apply* correctly?

Ⓐ Bears apply their thick fur.

Ⓑ The scary dream applied me awake.

Ⓒ The law against littering applies to everyone.

Ⓓ When the hikers apply the creek, they take off their shoes.

4. In which sentence could the word *applicable* be used to fill in the blank?

Ⓕ The picnic table was _____ and wide.

Ⓖ The bees were _____ in their hive.

Ⓗ Rules about table manners are always _____ when you are invited to dinner.

Ⓙ The musicians are _____ to the concert on Saturday night.

Writing Explain a rule you follow at home that is also *applicable* at school.
Use at least one of this week's words in your writing.

_____

_____

_____

_____

WEEK 16

inform • information
evidence • evident

Use the reproducible definitions on page 174 and the suggestions on page 6 to introduce the words for each day.

DAY 1

inform
(verb) To tell or give information to someone. *I will **inform** the school that you are ill.*

Say: *The verb **inform** is useful in many different kinds of situations. In fact, I just **informed** you of its importance. Think of how many times a day you tell someone something. Each time, you **inform** someone. If you tell me that you have done your homework, you have **informed** me.* Ask students to talk about a recent time in which they **informed** someone of something. Then have students complete the Day 1 activities on page 71. You may want to do the first one as a group.

DAY 2

information
(noun) Knowledge or facts about something. *Martin gathered **information** for his report on the planet Saturn.*

Say: *When we inform someone about something, we give him or her **information**.* Encourage students to think about the different categories of **information** by writing headings such as "scientific **information**," "math **information**," and "historical **information**" on the board. Ask students to give you pieces of **information** for each category, and list them under the headings. Then have students complete the Day 2 activities on page 71. You may want to do the first one as a group.

DAY 3

evidence
(noun) Information or facts that help prove something or make you believe that it is true. *Scientists are still looking for **evidence** of life on other planets.*

Students should be familiar with this term from science and detective fiction. Ask: *If you had baked cookies and discovered that they were gone from the plate, what **evidence** would you look for to determine who took them?* (e.g., crumbs on someone; the dog licking its lips) Then ask: *What types of jobs involve uncovering **evidence**?* (e.g., law enforcement; scientists) Have students complete the Day 3 activities on page 72. You may want to do the first one as a group.

DAY 4

evident
(adj.) Easy to see and understand; obvious. *It is **evident** from your test scores that you have been studying harder.*

Point out the similarity in the spelling of **evident** and "evidence." Say: *Something that is **evident** provides evidence that points to the truth of an idea or event.* Ask students to complete sentences using **evident**. For example: "It is **evident** that you have ___ (e.g., been working in the yard; just risen from bed) because ___." Then have students complete the Day 4 activities on page 72. You may want to do the first one as a group.

DAY 5

Have students complete page 73. Call on students to read aloud their answers to the writing activity.

**Daily
Academic
Vocabulary**

Day 1 | inform

1. How would you complete this sentence? Say it aloud to a partner.

I recently informed a friend that _____.

2. Which sentence does not use *inform* correctly? Circle your answer.

a. Please inform the president that I have received her message.

b. The sign informs drivers of the speed limit.

c. The encyclopedia entry informs me that Tokyo is the capital of Japan.

d. The inform on the sign-up sheet was confusing to me.

3. Which word means the same thing as *inform*? Circle your answer.

a. include   c. tell

b. insist   d. ask

Day 2 | information

1. How would you complete this sentence? Say it aloud to a partner.

I would like to find more information about _____.

2. List three pieces of *information* about your school.

a. _____

b. _____

c. _____

3. Which sentences use *information* correctly? Circle your answers.

a. He informations us about the history of the old whaling towns.

b. This Web site has the information about the movie we want to see.

c. The guide book contains information about the Freedom Trail.

d. When they information me about the tour, I'll let you know.

4. List three places you can find *information* about animals.

a. _____

b. _____

c. _____

**Daily
Academic
Vocabulary**

Day 3 | evidence

1. How would you complete this sentence? Say it aloud to a partner.

Looking in my bedroom would provide evidence that I like _____.

2. Suppose you bicycle to school one morning. After you get there, what would be three pieces of *evidence* that school had been canceled for the day?

a. _____

b. _____

c. _____

3. Which of these would <u>not</u> be considered *evidence* that humans have been on the moon? Circle your answer.

a. an astronaut's footprints on the moon

b. a rock that an astronaut took from the moon

c. a photo of an astronaut placing a flag on the moon

d. a cartoon about a man who goes to the moon with his dog

Day 4 | evident

1. How would you complete this sentence? Say it aloud to a partner.

It was evident to me that my friend had stayed up late because _____.

2. In which sentence is *evident* <u>not</u> used correctly? Circle your answer.

a. The audience's loud clapping made it evident that they liked the singer.

b. The evident must be collected carefully.

c. The girl's laughter made it evident that she liked the joke.

d. It was evident that they didn't like the movie since they left in the middle of it.

3. In which sentence could the word *evident* be used to fill in the blank? Circle your answer.

a. Her smiling face made it _____ that Kayla was unhappy.

b. Scientific _____ helps us understand our world.

c. Your complaints make it _____ that you would rather do something else.

d. Everything was _____ after he stopped wearing glasses.

Name_____

Day 5 inform • information • evidence • evident

Fill in the bubble next to the correct answer.

1. Which sentence uses the word *inform* correctly?

Ⓐ The librarian informed me that I need to return a book.

Ⓑ A careful gathering of inform is important for writing a good report.

Ⓒ The tickets informed us at the new baseball park.

Ⓓ The writer informed her new book.

2. For which of these activities would it be most important to gather *information*?

Ⓕ selling candy bars

Ⓖ giving a talk on healthy eating

Ⓗ walking home

Ⓙ wrapping a present with paper and ribbon

3. Which of the following might be *evidence* used to solve a crime?

Ⓐ fingerprints

Ⓑ good hearing

Ⓒ strong sense of smell

Ⓓ logical thinking

4. In which sentence is *evident* used correctly?

Ⓕ The researcher gathered evident.

Ⓖ Since the answer was evident, I wasn't sure what the answer was.

Ⓗ If you follow the clues, the solution is evident.

Ⓙ Staying out in the heat too long evident makes you tired.

Writing   Write about a time that you gathered *information* or *evidence*.
Why were you looking for it and what did you find? Use at least
two of this week's words in your writing.

_____

_____

_____

_____

develop • development

Use the reproducible definitions on page 175 and the suggestions on page 6 to introduce the words for each day.

DAY 1

develop
(verb) To make something more complete or effective. *The students will **develop** the homework assignment into a project for the science fair.*

Say: *It's satisfying to **develop** a small idea into something bigger. For example, I could notice that there is a new exhibit at the zoo and **develop** that thought into a field trip.* Ask students for examples of ideas or projects that they have **developed**. After responses, ask: *How did you develop that? What did you do to **develop** it?* Encourage students to use the word **develop** in their responses. Then have students complete the Day 1 activities on page 75. You may want to do the first one as a group.

DAY 2

develop
(verb) To grow or become stronger. *Small sand piles often **develop** into large sand dunes as a result of high winds.*

Say: *This definition of **develop** often refers to size or maturity.* Ask: *How does a tadpole **develop** into a frog?* (e.g., it grows; matures; grows legs) Then ask: *How might small bodies of water **develop** into larger ones?* (e.g., increased rainfall; dams being built) Then say: *People also **develop** from babies into adults.* Finally, have students complete the Day 2 activities on page 75. You may want to do the first one as a group.

DAY 3

development
(noun) The act or process of bringing something to a completed state. *I think your story needs further **development** before you turn it in.*

Say: *When you work to complete an assignment or a project, you work on its **development**.* Ask volunteers to describe the **development** of a project they have completed at school or outside of school. Then have students complete the Day 3 activities on page 76. You may want to do the first one as a group.

DAY 4

development
(noun) An important event or happening. *The newscaster announced the latest **development** in the story.*

Tell students that they often hear this word in connection with the news. Explain that when something new happens in an ongoing story, it is called a **development**. Say: *Everyday life can also have **developments**. For example, if you had to move or if an aunt came to visit for a month, this would be a new **development** in your family life. If someone donated computers to our computer lab, that would be an exciting **development** for our school.* Invite volunteers to talk about a recent **development** in their lives. Then have students complete the Day 4 activities on page 76. You may want to do the first one as a group.

DAY 5

Have students complete page 77. Call on students to read aloud their answers to the writing activity.

Name_____

Day 1 develop

1. How would you complete this sentence? Say it aloud to a partner.

I can develop an idea for a story by _____.

2. Which sentence uses *develop* correctly? Circle your answer.

   a. Did you develop the multiplication problem?
   b. I wrote a letter and put it in a develop.
   c. The committee will develop a plan for a recycling program.
   d. In the develop of this problem, I believe that the players are at fault.

3. Which phrase best completes this sentence? Circle your answer.

I will develop my collection of coins by _____.

   a. reading about collections
   b. reading a book about coins
   c. spending all my coins
   d. adding coins that I do not have

4. How can you *develop* a friendship?

_____

_____

Day 2 develop

1. How would you complete this sentence? Say it aloud to a partner.

An egg can develop into a _____.

2. Which sentence does <u>not</u> use *develop* correctly? Circle your answer.

   a. This seed will develop into a bean plant.
   b. Large clouds developed as the storm approached.
   c. As Seth got better, the rash slowly developed.
   d. The long-distance runner had to develop strong legs.

3. Which sentence describes something that is *developing?* Circle your answer.

   a. A new plant is growing from a seed.
   b. A pile of clothes is being washed.
   c. A group of students are waiting on the corner for the bus.
   d. A lightbulb is giving off light.

Day 3 development

1. How would you complete this sentence? Say it aloud to a partner.

I would like to work on the development of _____.

2. In which sentence would *development* <u>not</u> replace the underlined word? Circle your answer.

   a. They are working on the <u>completion</u> of a new road across town.

   b. The drama club is working on the <u>progress</u> of their new play.

   c. I enjoyed watching the <u>growth</u> of the bud into a flower.

   d. <u>Increase</u> your abilities to succeed at school and in your life.

3. List three steps in the *development* of an idea into a story.

   a. _____

   b. _____

   c. _____

Day 4 development

1. How would you complete this sentence? Say it aloud to a partner.

An exciting development in my life has been _____.

2. Which of these is an example of a plot *development* in a fairy tale? Circle your answer.

   a. "Grandma" suddenly reveals that she is really the Big Bad Wolf.

   b. The Big Bad Wolf has sharp teeth.

   c. Little Red Riding Hood wears a red hood.

   d. Grandma lives in the forest.

3. Which sentence uses *development* correctly? Circle your answer.

   a. In development, it is important to pay attention.

   b. I development a fear of spiders.

   c. The weather forecaster reported the latest developments in the storm.

   d. As the story developments, it gets more interesting.

Name _____

Day 5 **develop • development**

Fill in the bubble next to the correct answer.

1. Which sentence uses the word *develop* correctly?

Ⓐ The develop has not been successful.

Ⓑ A gifted writer can develop one event into a whole story.

Ⓒ Hayden's develop of pain in his shoulder means he can't play for the team.

Ⓓ The town's develop is growing every day.

2. Which sentence describes something that has <u>not</u> *developed*?

Ⓔ The caterpillar became a butterfly.

Ⓖ Jose can now lift 50 pounds.

Ⓗ The flower withered and died.

Ⓛ The storm became a hurricane.

3. Which of the following would <u>not</u> help in the *development* of a school project?

Ⓐ asking a teacher for help on the project

Ⓑ gathering information for the project

Ⓒ thinking about what you want to do on the project

Ⓓ forgetting to buy the supplies you need

4. Which of the following is an example of a plot *development* in a detective story?

Ⓔ The detective returns home to fix a broken chair.

Ⓖ The detective finds a fingerprint that may help solve the crime.

Ⓗ The detective is confused about what to cook.

Ⓛ The detective takes a nap because she is very tired.

Writing What new product would you like to invent? How would you *develop* it? Be sure to use the word *develop* in your writing.

_____

_____

_____

_____

CUMULATIVE REVIEW
WORDS FROM WEEKS 10–17

applicable
application
apply
assign
assignment
complex
complicate
complicated
complication
defend
delegate
designate
detail
develop
development
evidence
evident
in detail
inform
information
perspective
position
refer
reference
specific
specify
viewpoint

Days 1–4

Each day's activity is a cloze paragraph that students complete with words or forms of words that they have learned in weeks 10–17. Before students begin, pronounce each word in the box on the student page, have students repeat each word, and then review each word's meaning(s). **Other ways to review the words:**

- Start a sentence containing one of the words and have students finish the sentence orally. For example:

  *I think the most reliable **information** on world events comes from…*
  *I can speak **in detail** about…*

- Provide students with a definition and ask them to supply the word that fits it.

- Ask questions that require students to know the meaning of each word. For example:

  *How would you **defend** your **position** on school uniforms?*
  *What **specific** household task do you do at home every week?*

- Have students use each word in a sentence.

Day 5

Start by reviewing the words in the crossword puzzle activity for Day 5. Write the words on the board and have students repeat them after you. Provide a sentence for one of the words. Ask students to think of their own sentence and share it with a partner. Call on several students to share their sentences. Follow the same procedure for the remaining words. Then have students complete the crossword activity.

Extension Ideas

Use any of the following activities to help integrate the vocabulary words into other content areas:

- Have students **develop** a **reference** binder for new students that may join the class. What would those students need to know about the class and school?

- Have students decide on a writing **assignment** for the week that is **applicable** to what you are studying.

- Have students find **evidence** to support a scientific fact or theory you are studying.

- Have students trace the **development** of the wheel through time, searching for **evidence** on Web sites and in **reference** books.

Daily Academic Vocabulary

applicable	details	evidence	information	position
applications	development	in detail	informed	specific

Day 1

Fill in the blanks with words from the word box.

In 2006, many scientists changed their point of view. They took a new

_____ on the number of planets named in our solar system. It

was a _____ that resulted from scientists meeting to decide

on a new definition for "planet." They agreed to define a planet thoroughly and

_____ by its size, shape, and path of orbit. This was not good

for Pluto. It had been called a planet before, but because of its unusual orbit,

the new definition was not _____. This decision shows that as

scientists gain more knowledge and _____, something believed

to be a fact can change.

Day 2

Fill in the blanks with words from the word box.

A month ago, my teacher told us that we were going to have a debate. She

_____ us that we had to pick a particular invention and argue

its importance in history. My _____ invention was the wheel. A

wheel has many uses. Its _____ include moving bikes and cars

and being a small, but important, part of many other things. Wheels are necessary

_____ in watch and machine gears and are the basis of computer

disk drives and airplane turbines. Scientists have facts and _____

that wheels have existed for almost 6,000 years!

applied	complicated	designate	perspective
complex	defends	develop	specify

Day 3

Fill in the blanks with words from the word box.

The Lorax by Dr. Seuss is the book I name when someone asks me to

_____ my favorite book. The book seems easy to understand, but

it's actually fairly _____. There are two main characters who have

very different opinions. The Once-ler is a character who believes that it's okay to

_____, or choose, trees to be cut down to make clothes. The Lorax

is a creature who supports trees and _____ their right to live and

grow. Dr. Seuss uses a very clever plot in his book to make people think.

Day 4

Fill in the blanks with words from the word box.

Many people have strong views about video games. One _____

is that they set bad examples of behavior. Another view is that video games can be

_____ to education. Some information shows that video games build

hand-eye coordination and _____ other skills, such as finding solutions

to problems. Many parents and teachers believe that these findings don't include games

that are violent. The many opinions involved make video games a _____

topic. What are your views?

Name_____

Day 5

Crossword Challenge

For each clue, write one of the words from the word box to complete the puzzle.

assign
assignment
complicate
complication
delegate
evident
refer
reference
viewpoint

Down

1. a mention of someone or something
3. obvious
4. a way of thinking about something
6. to give as a task
7. to make something more difficult

Across

2. to give someone else the responsibility
5. to call attention to someone or something
8. a difficulty that causes a problem
9. a specific task given to someone

significance • significant
insignificant • emphasis • emphasize

Use the reproducible definitions on page 176 and the suggestions on page 6 to introduce the words for each day.

DAY 1

significance
(noun) The importance or meaning of something. *Everyone at the picnic table understood the significance of the darkening clouds.*

Say: *When something is important, it has significance. For example, school has significance because you learn the skills and knowledge you need for life.* Then say: *Many things can have significance. If I were to frown at you, what might be the significance of that frown? What could it mean? Why would it be important?* Then have students complete the Day 1 activities on page 83. You may want to do the first one as a group.

DAY 2

significant
(adj.) Important, or having great meaning. *The captain made the most significant contribution to the team.*

insignificant
(adj.) Not important, or having very little meaning. *The color of the bicycle is insignificant to the racer.*

Write "**significant**" and "**insignificant**" on the board. Ask students to identify the difference in spelling. Circle the prefix "in" and review its meaning. ("not" or "no") Ask: *What does insignificant mean?* ("not significant") Then say: *The same thing may be significant to one person and insignificant to another. A computer game might be significant to you, but insignificant to your parents.* Ask for other examples. Then have students complete the Day 2 activities on page 83. You may want to do the first one as a group.

DAY 3

emphasis
(noun) Special attention or importance given to something. *The history book's emphasis was on the causes of the war, not the results.*

Say: *Each school year, certain skills are given more attention than others. They are given emphasis. For example, in social studies for our grade, the emphasis is on ___. (e.g., our country's history) We give special attention to (our history) in our grade. In first grade math, the emphasis is on learning addition and subtraction facts.* Ask: *What is our emphasis in math right now? What is the emphasis in other subjects in our grade?* Then have students complete the Day 3 activities on page 84. You may want to do the first one as a group.

DAY 4

emphasize
(verb) To give emphasis or importance to something. *My parents emphasize the importance of good manners.*

Say: *When we give emphasis to something, we emphasize it. We give it importance. What do our school rules emphasize?* (e.g., fairness; sportsmanship) Then display a couple of magazine ads for products students know. Say: *Ads emphasize the important features of products.* Ask: *What do these ads emphasize about their products?* Then have students complete the Day 4 activities on page 84. You may want to do the first one as a group.

DAY 5

Have students complete page 85. Call on students to read aloud their answers to the writing activity.

Daily Academic Vocabulary

Day 1 significance

1. How would you complete this sentence? Say it aloud to a partner.

The significance of family is _____.

2. What is the *significance* of the fifty stars on the American flag? Circle your answer.

   a. They fill the upper left corner, which would otherwise be empty.
   b. The stars stand for all the stars in the Milky Way.
   c. Each star represents one of the fifty states.
   d. Each star is very pretty and decorative.

3. Which of the following is an event of *significance* in history? Circle your answer.

   a. the local basketball game
   b. Galileo Galilei inventing the thermometer
   c. the making of each telephone call
   d. doing your homework on the computer

4. What is something that has *significance* in your life?

_____

_____

Day 2 significant • insignificant

1. How would you complete these sentences? Say them aloud to a partner.

_____ plays a significant role in my life.

When I choose a friend, _____ is insignificant.

2. Which of these conditions would your doctor find *significant*? Circle your answers.

   a. high fever   c. broken fingernail
   b. dirty knees   d. itchy rash

3. Which one would be *insignificant* if you wanted to join a theater club? Circle your answer.

   a. your skill at pretending to be other people
   b. how tall you are
   c. your ability to remember all your lines
   d. how comfortable you feel in front of an audience

Day 3 emphasis

1. How would you complete this sentence? Say it aloud to a partner.

If I were in charge of our school, I would put more emphasis on _____.

2. Which statement would receive the most *emphasis* from a weather forecaster? Circle your answer.

    a. Today is Tuesday.

    b. The temperature remains steady.

    c. A major snowstorm is headed our way tomorrow.

    d. Stay tuned to hear more about the weekend forecast.

3. Which sentence does <u>not</u> use *emphasis* correctly? Circle your answer.

    a. The mayor tried to emphasis his point by speaking slowly.

    b. Place the emphasis on the most important idea.

    c. The emphasis in our P.E. program is on fair play.

    d. Our teacher places an emphasis on completing assignments on time.

Day 4 emphasize

1. How would you complete this sentence? Say it aloud to a partner.

My parents always emphasize the importance of _____.

2. Which ones would be important to *emphasize* in a speech asking others to recycle? Circle your answers.

    a. how recycling helps the environment

    b. how many trees are in the world

    c. endangered animals

    d. how easy it is to recycle

3. Imagine that you are writing an article. List two ways you could *emphasize* an important point.

    a. _____

    b. _____

Name_____

Day 5 | **significance • significant • insignificant**
emphasis • emphasize

Fill in the bubble next to the correct answer.

1. In which sentence could the word *significance* fill in the blank?

Ⓐ The brain is the _____ of our nervous system.

Ⓑ The scientist explained the _____ of the latest discovery.

Ⓒ They chose two athletes to _____ the country at the Olympics.

Ⓓ Cooperation is the _____ of making our team successful.

2. Which word is the best synonym for *significant*?

Ⓕ silly

Ⓖ confusing

Ⓗ important

Ⓙ eventful

3. Which of these is an *insignificant* part of the human body?

Ⓐ the heart

Ⓑ the lungs

Ⓒ the eyes

Ⓓ the earlobes

4. In which sentence could *emphasize* replace the underlined words?

Ⓕ Our gym teachers place importance on ways we can be active at home.

Ⓖ The dancers take turns practicing in front of the mirror.

Ⓗ The construction workers carefully lift the heavy beam into place.

Ⓙ The cooks rolled out the dough for the pie to be served for dessert.

Writing   What *significant* things in your life do you place an *emphasis* on? Use at least one of this week's words in your description.

_____

_____

_____

_____

condition • factor • aspect

Use the reproducible definitions on page 177 and the suggestions on page 6 to introduce the words for each day.

DAY 1

condition
(noun) The general state of being of someone or something. *You must return borrowed books in good condition.*

Tell students that we use this word to talk about people and things. Say: *When we talk about a person's condition, we are usually talking about their health.* Then ask: *What does a bicycle in "good condition" look like?* Then have students complete the Day 1 activities on page 87. You may want to do the first one as a group.

DAY 2

condition
(noun) Something that is needed before another thing can happen. *You may attend the carnival on the condition that you clean your room.*

Say: *You have probably heard someone say, "I'll do it on one condition."* Ask: *If I say, "I'll give the class a free period if everyone completes the assignment on time," what is the condition that needs to exist before the class can have a free period?* Students should see that completing the assignment on time is the **condition** that must be met. Then have students complete the Day 2 activities on page 87. You may want to do the first one as a group.

DAY 3

factor
(noun) Something that influences a result. *The weather was a factor in the outcome of the sailboat race.*

Say: *A factor is something that affects or influences how something happens. Yesterday we talked about a scenario in which I offered the class a free period on the condition that everyone completed an assignment on time.* Ask: *What factors might affect your ability to complete the assignment?* Then say: *Many situations or activities have factors that affect or determine their outcome.* Ask: *What factors might affect who wins a game? What factors might affect a plant's growth?* Then have students complete the Day 3 activities on page 88. You may want to do the first one as a group.

DAY 4

aspect
(noun) One particular feature or characteristic of something. *Consider every aspect of the problem before suggesting a solution.*

Say: *Frequently, things or ideas have many aspects or features. We sometimes put aspects into categories. For instance, someone might comment that a television program has educational aspects, such as that it teaches kindness. That same program might have entertaining aspects too, such as funny characters.* Then say: *Aspects can be positive or negative. What is a positive aspect of TV? A negative aspect?* Then have students complete the Day 4 activities on page 88. You may want to do the first one as a group.

DAY 5

Have students complete page 89. Call on students to read aloud their answers to the writing activity.

Name_____

Day 1 condition

1. How would you complete this sentence? Say it aloud to a partner.

You could describe the condition of my room at home as _____ because you'd see _____.

2. What should you do if your classroom is in bad *condition*? Circle your answer.

    a. Tell your teacher that she needs to clean the room.
    b. Leave your books and papers around the room.
    c. Help your classmates put things away.
    d. Watch as other people clean the room.

3. Which of these should an athlete do if the coach tells her to get in better *condition*? Circle your answers.

    a. eat healthy foods
    b. watch more television
    c. buy a new computer game
    d. exercise regularly

I always keep my feathers in good condition.

Day 2 condition

1. How would you complete this sentence? Say it aloud to a partner.

I would agree to _____, but only on the condition that _____.

2. Which sentences use *condition* correctly? Circle your answers.

    a. If this condition is not met, you will not be allowed to enter the contest.
    b. I condition that tomorrow will be a better day for the trip.
    c. Because she met the conditions for admission, she will be a student at the new school.
    d. In conditions, cats will sleep sixteen hours a day.

3. Which one is <u>not</u> a *condition* for checking out a library book? Circle your answer.

    a. You will keep the book in good condition.
    b. You will return the book on time.
    c. You will not lose the book.
    d. You will finish reading the book.

Daily Academic Vocabulary

Day 3 factor

1. How would you complete this sentence? Say it aloud to a partner.

The most important factor in choosing an after-school activity is _____.

2. Which of these would be a *factor* in deciding to do a report on a particular topic? Circle your answers.

    a. You are interested in the topic.

    b. You can't find any books on the topic.

    c. You already know a little about the topic.

    d. The topic is not on the list approved by your teacher.

3. List three *factors* that contribute to an enjoyable field trip.

    a. _____

    b. _____

    c. _____

Day 4 aspect

1. How would you complete this sentence? Say it aloud to a partner.

The aspect of summer vacation that I enjoy the most is _____.

2. Which word is a synonym for *aspect*? Circle your answer.

    a. wonder   c. negative

    b. feature   d. problem

3. Which sentences do <u>not</u> use *aspect* correctly? Circle your answers.

    a. I studied every aspect of the dinosaur skeleton.

    b. In the aspect, travelers gather to await the arrival of the train.

    c. A noticeable aspect of his speech was the frequent use of the word "awesome."

    d. Farmers aspect their crops before the first frost.

4. What *aspects* of school do you enjoy the most?

_____

_____

Day 5 condition • factor • aspect

Fill in the bubble next to the correct answer.

1. In which sentence could the word *condition* fill in the blank?

Ⓐ The fans in the stadium roared their _____.

Ⓑ If the _____ agrees, we can spend a week at the lake.

Ⓒ To keep the equipment in good working _____, clean it after every use.

Ⓓ If my _____ crashes, I cannot complete my homework.

2. Which one is most likely to be a *condition* for lending your friend your bicycle?

Ⓕ Your friend rides the bicycle to the library.

Ⓖ Your friend decorates the bicycle.

Ⓗ Your friend says the bicycle is cool.

Ⓙ Your friend returns the bicycle before you need to use it next.

3. Which sentence does <u>not</u> use *factor* correctly?

Ⓐ The actor on the stage factored his lines.

Ⓑ The difficulty of finding materials was a factor in deciding to halt our project.

Ⓒ Hard work is always a factor in success.

Ⓓ Height is often a factor in basketball.

4. Which of the following is <u>not</u> an *aspect* of mystery stories?

Ⓕ a trail of clues

Ⓖ rhyming words

Ⓗ a crime or strange event

Ⓙ a suspect

Writing   Write about an interesting *aspect* of your school or town. Be sure to use at least one of this week's words in your writing.

_____

_____

_____

_____

WEEK 21

modify • modification
substitute

Use the reproducible definitions on page 178 and the suggestions on page 6 to introduce the words for each day.

DAY 1

modify
(verb) To change or alter somewhat. *I will **modify** the dialogue in my story to make it sound more realistic.*

Say: *When we use the word **modify** to talk about changing something, we are usually talking about a small change, not a large one. For example, if I were building a house and I **modified** the plans, I might change the size of the living room windows. I would not do something major such as decide to add a second floor.* Ask: *What are things you might **modify** in your writing throughout the writing process? What things would you **modify** in our classroom?* Then have students complete the Day 1 activities on page 91. You may want to do the first one as a group.

DAY 2

modification
(noun) A change or alteration of something. *The teacher's **modification** of the assignment made it easier to complete.*

Say: *When we modify something, the result is called a **modification**.* Invite students to suggest a **modification** to the school's lunch program. Then ask: *What **modifications** have been made to our town recently?* (e.g., new roads; buildings; stores) *What **modifications** would you make to our school building?* Then have students complete the Day 2 activities on page 91. You may want to do the first one as a group.

DAY 3

substitute
(verb) To put in the place of another person or thing. *The coach will **substitute** the rookie for the injured player.*

Ask students to describe situations in which they might need to **substitute** one thing or person for another. Ask: *For instance, if the electricity fails, what would you **substitute** for the reading lamp you were using? What would you **substitute** if your pen ran out of ink? In what other instances do you **substitute** one thing for another?* Then have students complete the Day 3 activities on page 92. You may want to do the first one as a group.

DAY 4

substitute
(noun) Someone or something that takes the place of another. *My aunt uses honey in her tea as a **substitute** for sugar.*

Say: *When we substitute one thing or person for another, we use a **substitute**. Even though the **substitute** may not be exactly the same, it is important that it be able to perform the same function.* Ask: *What role does a **substitute** teacher take in a classroom? What would a **substitute** for a pencil need to do? Name some **substitutes** for a pencil.* Name other items and have students brainstorm **substitutes**. (e.g., fork; glass; napkin) Then have students complete the Day 4 activities on page 92. You may want to do the first one as a group.

DAY 5

Have students complete page 93. Call on students to read aloud their answers to the writing activity.

Daily
Academic
Vocabulary

Day 1 modify

1. How would you complete this sentence? Say it aloud to a partner.

I would like to modify _____ because _____.

2. Which sentence describes someone *modifying* something? Circle your answer.

    a. The wrecking crew uses dynamite to destroy the building.

    b. Deborah changed the title of her story to make it more mysterious.

    c. The flood swept away everything in its path.

    d. Every evening I read the headlines in the newspaper.

3. Which words are synonyms for *modify*? Circle your answers.

    a. alter   c. stay

    b. wound   d. change

Day 2 modification

1. How would you complete this sentence? Say it aloud to a partner.

One modification of our school schedule should be _____.

2. Which sentence does not use *modification* correctly? Circle your answer.

    a. The modification to the car's engine improved its performance.

    b. Sam suggested a modification to the exercise routine.

    c. The modification of the amusement park ride made it safer.

    d. The modification of one athlete for another made our team stronger.

3. Which one is not an example of a *modification*? Circle your answer.

    a. putting a book into large type for people with vision problems

    b. adding a page at the end of a book to tell about the author

    c. adding a new book to a series of books about a detective

    d. putting a book on tape so readers can read along with the narrator

4. What *modifications* would you make to your textbooks to make them better?

_____

_____

_____

Daily Academic Vocabulary

Day 3 | **substitute**

---

1. How would you complete this sentence? Say it aloud to a partner.

My diet would be more healthy if I would substitute _____ for _____.

2. What would happen if I *substituted* the number 10 for the number 8 in this example: 125 x 8 = 1,000? Circle your answers.

   a. The product would change.

   b. The product would remain the same.

   c. The product would be less than 1,000.

   d. The product would be more than 1,000.

3. Which sentence uses *substitute* correctly? Circle your answer.

   a. I substituted my dog in water when it was dirty.

   b. Terry substituted blueberries for cranberries in these muffins.

   c. In the substitute of the building, you will find a deep elevator shaft.

   d. Nina did not want to substitute herself to the hot, humid weather.

Day 4 | **substitute**

---

1. How would you complete this sentence? Say it aloud to a partner.

_____ would be a good substitute for _____.

2. What is always true about a *substitute*? Circle your answer.

   a. It is a copy of the original.

   b. It is better than the original.

   c. It is not as good as the original.

   d. It can do what the original does.

3. Read this quotation. Then list four *substitutes* for the word "said."

"I need help on this project," <u>said</u> Chris.

   a. _____

   b. _____

   c. _____

   d. _____

Name_____

Day 5 **modify • modification • substitute**

Fill in the bubble next to the correct answer.

1. Which sentence uses *modify* correctly?

Ⓐ The student modifies when he does not know the answer.

Ⓑ My sister modified the sweater by sewing on different buttons.

Ⓒ The modify did not please everyone on the committee.

Ⓓ Craig and I modify every weekend at the skating rink.

2. In which sentence could *modification* replace the underlined word or words?

Ⓕ The change I made in the first paragraph improved my essay.

Ⓖ Tamara presented an interesting explanation of the problem.

Ⓗ The carpenter used a tape measure to determine the length of the board.

Ⓙ The struggle with the jammed door frustrated James.

3. Which one is not an example of someone *substituting* one thing for another?

Ⓐ Zoe took out her contact lenses and put on her glasses.

Ⓑ When he ran out of bricks, he used stones to make the wall higher.

Ⓒ Ginny gathered small sticks for starting the campfire.

Ⓓ Because he forgot his umbrella, Perry held a newspaper over his head.

4. If your parents went out for the evening, who would be the best *substitute* for them?

Ⓕ your friend

Ⓖ a trusted sitter

Ⓗ your younger sibling

Ⓙ a lion tamer

Writing   Write about a time you *modified* your plans for a day. Be sure to use one of this week's words in your writing.

_____

_____

_____

_____

Daily Academic Vocabulary

pattern • imitate • imitation

Use the reproducible definitions on page 179 and the suggestions on page 6 to introduce the words for each day.

DAY 1

pattern
(verb) To make something or to act following a plan or a model. *The best dancers* **pattern** *their steps after Ms. Petrie's example.*

Display a print or a piece of artwork. Say: *If I asked you to* **pattern** *your own artwork after this piece, what would you do?* Then say: *Someone might choose to* **pattern** *his or her life after the life of someone they admire.* Ask: *On whose life might you choose to* **pattern** *yours?* Then have students complete the Day 1 activities on page 95. You may want to do the first one as a group.

DAY 2

imitate
(verb) To copy the actions or appearance of something or someone. *My little brother* **imitates** *everything I do.*

Ask: *Has anyone with little sisters or brothers been annoyed by the way they* **imitate** *what you do? What specific things do they do?* After students have offered some examples, tell them that while we can **imitate** other people, we can also make things that **imitate** other things. Say: *For example, animators create figures that* **imitate** *the movements of real people.* Invite volunteers to offer additional examples. Then have students complete the Day 2 activities on page 95. You may want to do the first one as a group.

DAY 3

imitation
(noun) The act of imitating or copying. *His* **imitation** *of a monkey is very funny.*

Say: *When we imitate, that act of copying is called an* **imitation**. *When your little sister imitates your actions, she is doing an* **imitation** *of you.* Ask: *When have you seen or done an* **imitation** *of someone?* Make sure students' responses pertain to this definition, not the definition for Day 4. Ask: *Have you ever heard the saying "***Imitation** *is the sincerest form of flattery"? What do you think that means?* Then have students complete the Day 3 activities on page 96. You may want to do the first one as a group.

DAY 4

imitation
(noun) A copy or likeness of something else. *Kayli saw an* **imitation** *of the Eiffel Tower in Paris, TN.*

Tell students that when a thing is copied, the result is called an **imitation**. Ask: *What are some* **imitations** *that you've seen?* Make sure their responses pertain to this definition, not the definition for Day 3. Students will probably be familiar with products that are **imitations** of famous brands of jeans and sneakers. Ask: *What are the differences between an original and an* **imitation**? Then have students complete the Day 4 activities on page 96. You may want to do the first one as a group.

DAY 5

Have students complete page 97. Call on students to read aloud their answers to the writing activity.

Name _____

Day 1 | pattern

1. How would you complete this sentence? Say it aloud to a partner.

When it comes to _____, I would like to pattern the actions of _____.

2. Chimpanzees sometimes *pattern* their behavior after humans. What does that mean? Circle your answer.

    a. Chimpanzees sometimes trace the outlines of humans.

    b. Humans often act like chimpanzees.

    c. Chimpanzees observe humans and copy some of their behaviors.

    d. Chimpanzees often follow humans in a line.

3. Which sentence uses *pattern* correctly? Circle your answer.

    a. Linda patterns around the lake in her rowboat.

    b. He patterned his Web page after his cousin's.

    c. The rain patterned on the pavement as we walked.

    d. She will pattern on the piano until she masters that piece.

4. When have you *patterned* your actions after someone else's?

_____

_____

Day 2 | imitate

1. How would you complete this sentence? Say it aloud to a partner.

It is not always good to imitate someone else because _____.

2. Which word is a synonym for *imitate*? Circle your answer.

    a. start   c. copy

    b. teach   d. insult

3. If you are told to *imitate* the way someone delivers a speech, what should you do? Circle your answer.

    a. speak the way that person does

    b. read a book on giving speeches

    c. learn to speak in another language

    d. tell the speaker what he did wrong

Parrots **imitate** human speech!

Name_____

Daily
Academic
Vocabulary

Day 3 imitation

1. How would you complete this sentence? Say it aloud to a partner.

I know someone who does a great imitation of _____.

2. Which sentence describes an *imitation*? Circle your answer.

    a. The comedian copies the famous actor's facial expressions exactly.

    b. The artist ignores what all the other artists have done and finds her own style.

    c. The boy looks at himself in the mirror as he combs his hair.

    d. Kate stays up late into the night to finish reading the book.

3. Which one is probably an *imitation* of human speech? Circle your answer.

    a. a bird chirping   c. a monkey howling

    b. a baby babbling   d. a tiger growling

4. Why do you think people do *imitations*?

_____

_____

Day 4 imitation

1. How would you complete this sentence? Say it aloud to a partner.

I wish I had an imitation of _____.

2. Which one is the opposite of an *imitation*? Circle your answer.

    a. a likeness   c. a copy

    b. a reproduction   d. an original

3. A woman lost what she thinks is a diamond necklace, but it is only an *imitation*. Which phrases best describe what the woman lost? Circle your answers.

    a. expensive jewelry   c. something valuable

    b. a fake diamond necklace d. something of little worth

Name _____

Day 5 pattern • imitate • imitation

Fill in the bubble next to the correct answer.

1. **Which sentence describes someone who *patterns* their behavior on someone else's?**

   Ⓐ Arlene has created a very unusual portrait of Sam.

   Ⓑ That girl has a style all of her own.

   Ⓒ Thomas chooses to eat the candy that nobody else likes.

   Ⓓ Before acting, Kevin always asks himself what Carmen would do.

2. **Why would a football player choose to *imitate* the throwing style of another quarterback?**

   Ⓕ That quarterback is about to retire.

   Ⓖ That quarterback wins every game.

   Ⓗ That quarterback is a good team player.

   Ⓙ Nobody likes the way that quarterback throws.

3. **In which sentence could *imitation* be used to fill in the blank?**

   Ⓐ The parrot _____ other birds and people.

   Ⓑ The child's _____ of her father's driving was comical.

   Ⓒ Because of the _____, I could not attend the party last night.

   Ⓓ The teachers _____ at the meeting with parents.

4. **Which sentence uses *imitation* correctly?**

   Ⓕ Farik's imitation of the famous actor was very convincing.

   Ⓖ The sloth imitations a tree because it moves so slowly.

   Ⓗ Stuart used a very different color and new style to make his imitation.

   Ⓙ It would be best not to imitation but to find your own style.

Writing   Write about something you have learned by *imitating* what you've seen someone else do. Use at least one of this week's words in your writing.

_____

_____

_____

_____

Daily Academic Vocabulary

accurate • accuracy
precise • precision

Use the reproducible definitions on page 180 and the suggestions on page 6 to introduce the words for each day.

DAY 1

accurate
(adj.) Correct or free from errors. *Consult the atlas for accurate information on the mountain's height.*

accuracy
(noun) The condition of being exact and correct. *A good newspaper reporter checks the accuracy of her information.*

Say: *When something is accurate, each of its details are correct.* Ask: *Where do you expect to find the most accurate information about current events?* (e.g., newspapers; television; radio) *When is a painting of someone accurate?* Then tell students that a synonym for **accuracy** is "correctness." Ask: *What are some instances when accuracy is needed in schoolwork? How do you check your work for accuracy?* Encourage students to use the words **accurate** and **accuracy** in their responses. Then have students complete the Day 1 activities on page 99. You may want to do the first one as a group.

DAY 2

precise
(adj.) Very accurate or exact; definite. *The schedule tells you the precise time that the train will leave the station.*

Say: *When something is precise, it is as specific and accurate as possible. For example, while it might be accurate to say that it is hot outside, it would be precise to say that the temperature is 102 degrees.* Ask students for examples of situations in which it is important not only to be accurate, but also **precise**. (e.g., measuring medicine; adding up a bill; giving directions; recipes) Then have students complete the Day 2 activities on page 99. You may want to do the first one as a group.

DAY 3

precise
(adj.) Clearly said or communicated. *His precise response answered the judge's questions.*

Say: *Someone who chooses her words carefully and pronounces them carefully is being precise in her speech.* Ask students these "yes" or "no" questions: *If you are precise when you answer a question, do you give a long, drawn out answer? Or, do you answer briefly and accurately? Is your answer sure and definite? Or, do you say a lot but never really answer the question?* Then have students complete the Day 3 activities on page 100. You may want to do the first one as a group.

DAY 4

precision
(noun) Accuracy or exactness. *The marching band performed every step of the routine with precision.*

Say: *When you are precise, you have precision.* Ask: *When is it important to have precision in school?* (e.g., answers on tests; science experiments) Then have students complete the Day 4 activities on page 100. You may want to do the first one as a group.

DAY 5

Have students complete page 101. Call on students to read aloud their answers to the writing activity.

Daily Academic Vocabulary • EMC 2761 • © Evan-Moor Corporation

Name_____

Day 1 accurate • accuracy

1. How would you complete these sentences? Say them aloud to a partner.

It is important to be accurate when _____.

Accuracy in history books is important because _____.

2. The weather forecast you heard was <u>not</u> *accurate*. What happened to you as a result? Circle your answer.

    a. You were well prepared with the proper gear.

    b. You got soaked because you didn't know that you would need an umbrella.

    c. You were warm and comfortable waiting for the bus.

    d. Your boots protected your feet.

3. Which sentences use *accuracy* correctly? Circle your answers.

    a. The accuracy of the story has been checked and confirmed.

    b. You cannot trust the information on that Web site because it is accuracy.

    c. Because the artist drew her with accuracy, I recognized my friend right away.

    d. Be accuracy when you are measuring the window for curtains.

Day 2 precise

1. How would you complete this sentence? Say it aloud to a partner.

The precise location of my desk is _____.

2. Which word is a synonym for *precise*? Circle your answer.

    a. almost   c. exact

    b. close   d. wrong

3. Which sentence contains a *precise* measurement? Circle your answer.

    a. It is about 5 miles from our school to my house.

    b. I walked a few blocks with my dog.

    c. The crowd drank nearly 10 gallons of water.

    d. My dad is 5 feet and 10½ inches tall.

4. What is the *precise* number of students in your classroom?

_____

I have 8 toes, to be **precise**.

Daily
Academic
Vocabulary

Day 3 precise

1. How would you complete this sentence? Say it aloud to a partner.

A time when it is important to be precise is when _____.

2. Which directions are *precise*? Circle your answer.

   a. The park is that way a bit.
   b. When you get close to the park, you'll see a tall building.
   c. The park is either by the library or city hall.
   d. To reach the park, drive north to the second traffic light, turn left, and go three blocks.

3. What should you do if your teacher asks you to be more *precise* in your report?

_____

_____

_____

_____

Day 4 precision

1. How would you complete this sentence? Say it aloud to a partner.

Precision is important when _____.

2. Which sentences use *precision* correctly? Circle your answers.

   a. Laugh loudly and with precision.
   b. The ship was off course because the navigation equipment lacked precision.
   c. The crooked lines in the child's drawing give it precision.
   d. The watchmaker guaranteed the precision of every watch he produced.

3. If you want to draw a straight line with *precision,* which tool would you use?
Circle your answer.

   a. scissors   c. screwdriver
   b. ruler   d. compass

Day 5 accurate • accuracy • precise • precision

Fill in the bubble next to the correct answer.

1. Which word would best describe an *accurate* answer?

Ⓐ false

Ⓑ wrong

Ⓒ correct

Ⓓ mistaken

2. Which sentence describes someone who is working to improve his or her *accuracy*?

Ⓕ Emily fell asleep with her head on her math book.

Ⓖ Dale let his paintbrush drift over the canvas.

Ⓗ The man lazily dangled the fishing line as he whistled a tune.

Ⓙ Jamie carefully focused on the basket before shooting the ball.

3. Which sentence uses *precise* correctly?

Ⓐ I will get up tomorrow at just about the precise time the sun rises.

Ⓑ The precise width of the board is 4 inches.

Ⓒ The precise day that Karen will arrive is Saturday or Sunday.

Ⓓ I rounded up the numbers and estimated the precise answer.

4. In which sentence could *precision* replace the underlined word?

Ⓕ The <u>exactness</u> of the measurements helped her build a well-made cabinet.

Ⓖ Her <u>encouragement</u> gave me the confidence I needed to succeed.

Ⓗ The hikers climbed with <u>determination</u> to the top of the mountain.

Ⓙ The <u>depth</u> of this lake makes it a dangerous place to swim.

Writing Give a *precise* answer to this question: How does studying academic vocabulary help you in school? Be sure to use at least one of this week's words in your writing.

_____

_____

_____

_____

primary • dominant • prevalent

Use the reproducible definitions on page 181 and the suggestions on page 6 to introduce the words for each day.

DAY 1

primary
(adj.) Most important; main or chief. *The **primary** reason for choosing that jacket was its affordability.*

Say: *If I say that I have several reasons for doing something but one "**primary** reason," I mean that one reason is more important than the others.* Ask students to list the reasons they have for wanting to do well in school, in sports, or in another activity. Then ask them to decide which of those reasons is the **primary** one. Have students complete the Day 1 activities on page 103. You may want to do the first one as a group.

DAY 2

primary
(adj.) First in order or time. *When you start school, you are in the **primary** grades.*

Say: *When we put things in order, the thing that comes first is the **primary** thing.* Ask students to describe what they might do in the **primary** stage of working on a project. (e.g., decide on a topic; make a list of things to do or materials needed) Then have students complete the Day 2 activities on page 103. You may want to do the first one as a group.

DAY 3

dominant
(adj.) Most powerful or important. *The **dominant** animal in the herd will eat before the others.*

Ask students what could make one animal in a herd or pack be the **dominant** animal. Students might mention age, physical strength, intelligence, etc. Tell students that a feature of a person or a thing that stands out is called the **dominant** feature. Say: *For instance, Abraham Lincoln's height could be considered his **dominant** physical characteristic. His **dominant** personality feature might have been his honesty or humor.* Ask: *Can you name the **dominant** characteristics or features of any famous people, living or dead?* Encourage students to use the word **dominant** in their responses. Then have students complete the Day 3 activities on page 104. You may want to do the first one as a group.

DAY 4

prevalent
(adj.) Found or happening frequently; widespread. *The cold virus is **prevalent** in the winter months.*

Tell students that when something is **prevalent** it happens often or is seen often. Invite students to think about their neighborhoods. Ask: *What kinds of buildings are **prevalent** where you live?* (e.g., apartment buildings; houses; skyscrapers) Then have students complete the Day 4 activities on page 104. You may want to do the first one as a group.

DAY 5

Have students complete page 105. Call on students to read aloud their answers to the writing activity.

**Daily
Academic
Vocabulary**

Day 1 primary

1. **How would you complete this sentence? Say it aloud to a partner.**

   My primary interest outside of school is _____.

2. **Which of these is the *primary* reason to attend school? Circle your answer.**

   a. School teaches knowledge and skills useful for a productive life.
   b. There are friends and games at school.
   c. Being at home all the time would be boring.
   d. If you didn't go to school, you could play all day.

3. **Which sentence does <u>not</u> use *primary* correctly? Circle your answer.**

   a. The primary purpose of this assignment is to improve your spelling.
   b. Good preparation for a test is of primary importance.
   c. We will primary the list of things to do.
   d. My primary concern is your safety.

4. **If you were an astronaut on the space shuttle, what might be a *primary* objective you would have for the mission?**

   _____

   _____

Day 2 primary

1. **How would you complete this sentence? Say it aloud to a partner.**

   The primary step of doing a science experiment is to _____.

2. **Which sentences use *primary* correctly? Circle your answers.**

   a. In its primary, the tree sheds its leaves.
   b. A tadpole is a frog in its primary stage of development.
   c. The primary election is held before the regular election.
   d. After the first step in the process, we move on to the primary step.

3. **In the *primary* stage of the writing process, what do you do?**

   _____

   _____

Day 3 dominant

1. How would you complete this sentence? Say it aloud to a partner.

My dominant characteristic is _____.

2. How does a *dominant* person act in a group? List three things a *dominant* person might do.

a. _____

b. _____

c. _____

3. The importance of loyalty is the *dominant* theme of your essay. What did you do? Circle your answer.

a. You spent more time writing about loyalty than other ideas.

b. You wrote a story about winning a contest.

c. You wrote about the foods that you don't like.

d. You spent very little time writing about loyalty.

Day 4 prevalent

1. How would you complete this sentence? Say it aloud to a partner.

_____ is a prevalent topic of conversation among my friends.

2. Which sentence uses *prevalent* correctly? Circle your answer.

a. Danny's prevalent behavior at the dinner table was annoying.

b. The prevalent leader faces many challenges.

c. A prevalent adventure usually ends badly.

d. Spelling errors are prevalent in this paper.

3. List three *prevalent* opinions about your school.

a. _____

b. _____

c. _____

Flying is **prevalent** among parrots!

Name_____

Day 5 primary • dominant • prevalent

Fill in the bubble next to the correct answer.

1. In which sentence is *primary* <u>not</u> used correctly?

Ⓐ The primary source of information for my report will be an encyclopedia.

Ⓑ Ramona Quimby is the primary character in a series of popular books.

Ⓒ Automobile exhaust is the primary source of air pollution in many places.

Ⓓ I ignored the question because I thought it was primary.

2. In which sentence could *primary* replace the underlined word?

Ⓕ Our first teeth can also be called our <u>baby</u> teeth.

Ⓖ On an <u>ordinary</u> Saturday, I clean my room.

Ⓗ Many historians believe that the battle was <u>insignificant</u>.

Ⓙ The speaker ended her speech with <u>humorous</u> remarks.

3. Which word would most likely be used to describe a *dominant* person?

Ⓐ weak

Ⓑ fearful

Ⓒ powerful

Ⓓ shy

4. In which sentence is *prevalent* used correctly?

Ⓕ The vice president holds a prevalent position in our government.

Ⓖ Saturn is the most prevalent planet in the solar system.

Ⓗ The mosquito is a prevalent pest in the summer.

Ⓙ The morning is a prevalent time of day.

Writing What things or actions are *prevalent* in your school? Be sure to use the word *prevalent* in your writing.

_____

_____

_____

_____

criticism • critique • critical

Use the reproducible definitions on page 182 and the suggestions on page 6 to introduce the words for each day.

DAY 1

criticism
(noun) The act of judging what is good or bad in something. *The criticism offered by my writing group helped me make my story more interesting.*

Say: *Sometimes the word criticism means to only find fault with something.* Give an example. Then say: *In our use today, criticism will mean the act of pointing out both the good and the bad parts of something. When criticism helps someone to make improvements, we call it constructive criticism. Constructive criticism can help us correct wrong or ineffective ways of doing something.* Ask: *When have you been helped by constructive criticism?* Then have students complete the Day 1 activities on page 107. You may want to do the first one as a group.

DAY 2

critique
(verb) To say what is good or bad about something. *My older sister often critiques my reports.*

Say: *When teachers critique your work, they provide criticism. They want to mention the positive, as well as the negative, aspects.* Then ask: *If a reader critiques a book, what would that reader mention about the book? Besides schoolwork or a book, what are some other things that we could critique?* (e.g., movies; restaurants; music; sports teams) Then have students complete the Day 2 activities on page 107. You may want to do the first one as a group.

DAY 3

critical
(adj.) Very important or serious. *The right kind of cold weather gear is critical for people who live in the arctic regions.*

Say: *When someone is in critical condition, he or she is very seriously ill or injured. If a situation or a problem is critical, it is very important or on the brink of disaster.* Ask: *If your teacher says that following the directions on the test is critical, what do you think will happen if you don't follow the directions?* (e.g., do poorly or fail) Then have students complete the Day 3 activities on page 108. You may want to do the first one as a group.

DAY 4

critical
(adj.) Involving careful evaluation and judgment. *The boy used critical thinking skills to solve the problem.*

Say: *Critical can also describe the use of careful evaluation. A critical piece of writing would be one in which the writer has carefully examined and evaluated the subject.* Say: *You've probably heard the term critical thinking. Tell me whether each of these statements describes something a critical thinker does: makes a good guess; analyzes the facts; examines all the evidence; believes the first answer he hears.* Then have students complete the Day 4 activities on page 108. You may want to do the first one as a group.

DAY 5

Have students complete page 109. Call on students to read aloud their answers to the writing activity.

Name_____

Day 1 | criticism

1. How would you complete this sentence? Say it aloud to a partner.

A time when criticism of my work was helpful was _____.

2. Which sentences use *criticism* correctly? Circle your answers.

   a. The teacher provided written criticism of our project.
   b. Don't criticism his story.
   c. The skater listened to her coach's criticism of her routine.
   d. I was chosen to criticism the artwork.

3. Which of these illustrate *criticism*? Circle your answer.

The music teacher said, "_____."

   a. I hope you will practice every day this week
   b. You'll have fun playing this new song
   c. The first two songs were excellent, but you need to work on the third one
   d. Your lesson next week will be after school on Thursday

4. How can *criticism* help you to improve?

_____

_____

Day 2 | critique

1. How would you complete this sentence? Say it aloud to a partner.

I would critique the book _____ by saying that I liked _____, but not _____.

2. If you *critiqued* a painting in your art class, what would you be doing?
Circle your answers.

   a. picking out the best frame for it   c. pointing out its weaknesses
   b. pointing out its strengths   d. copying the painting

3. In which sentences is *critique* used correctly? Circle your answers.

   a. I critiqued the band concert for our school newspaper.
   b. That table covered with dust in the corner is a critique.
   c. My friend critiques my essays for me, showing me how I might improve them.
   d. The floor critiqued under the weight of the grand piano.

Daily Academic Vocabulary

Day 3 critical

1. How would you complete this sentence? Say it aloud to a partner.

I think a critical skill all adults need is _____.

2. The coach says that Nancy is a *critical* member of the team. What does that mean? Circle your answer.

   a. She always forgets the rules.
   b. She is too quick to make a decision.
   c. She is very important to the team's success.
   d. She never gets to practice on time.

3. Which words are synonyms for *critical*? Circle your answers.

   a. important   c. confusing
   b. possible   d. serious

4. What is *critical* to your success in school?

_____

_____

Day 4 critical

1. How would you complete this sentence? Say it aloud to a partner.

I use critical thinking skills to help me in _____.

2. When you produce a *critical* analysis of a poem, what do you do? Circle your answers.

   a. examine the poem   c. rewrite the poem
   b. recite the poem   d. judge the poem

3. Which sentence uses the word *critical* correctly? Circle your answer.

   a. The veterinarian made a critical examination of the injured dog.
   b. He is making a critical of the condition of the classroom.
   c. After he criticaled my essay, he turned his attention to my drawing.
   d. It criticals your performance if you do not study.

Name_____

Day 5 **criticism • critique • critical**

Fill in the bubble next to the correct answer.

1. In which sentence could *criticism* replace the underlined word or words?

Ⓐ Coach Davis offered to <u>talk to me</u> about my batting technique.

Ⓑ Our teacher <u>instructed</u> us to number our papers to twenty.

Ⓒ Dad tasted the soup and said <u>it needed more salt</u>.

Ⓓ After listening to my writing group's <u>comments and suggestions</u>, I revised the ending of my story.

2. Which sentence does <u>not</u> use *critique* correctly?

Ⓕ I asked the choir director to critique my singing.

Ⓖ At the critique moment, the player failed to catch the ball.

Ⓗ Students critique the food in the cafeteria at lunchtime.

Ⓙ My older brother hates it when our father critiques his driving.

3. In which sentence could the word *critical* fill in the blank?

Ⓐ Write an essay about the _____ of the environment.

Ⓑ The _____ is posted on our school's Web site.

Ⓒ Tomorrow the principal will _____ our projects.

Ⓓ It is _____ that you speak clearly in the spelling bee.

Will you **critique** my report?

4. Which sentence would <u>not</u> describe a *critical* person?

Ⓕ The judge carefully considered the argument from both sides.

Ⓖ Amir wrote out his plan of action and then revised it.

Ⓗ Julie bought the first car she drove.

Ⓙ The scientist conducted the experiment 18 times.

Writing What does *critical* reading mean? Be sure to use the word *critical* in your writing.

_____

_____

_____

_____

address • focus • topic

Use the reproducible definitions on page 183 and the suggestions on page 6 to introduce the words for each day.

DAY 1

address
(verb) To deal with a problem or situation. *I will **address** my problem of getting to school on time by getting up earlier.*

Say: *When you **address** a problem, you turn your attention to it and do something about it.* Ask students to give examples of problems or situations that they have **addressed**. Make sure they are problems that have been dealt with. Then have students complete the Day 1 activities on page 111. You may want to do the first one as a group.

DAY 2

address
(verb) To give a talk or speech. *The principal will **address** the students at today's assembly.*

Say: ***Address** can also mean to talk or give a speech to. Often, this refers to a formal or serious situation.* Ask: *Have you ever heard the phrase "The president will **address** the nation"? What does that mean?* Ask: *Who are examples of other people who must often **address** groups of people?* (e.g., politicians; teachers) *When might you be asked to **address** a group?* Have students complete the Day 2 activities on page 111. You may want to do the first one as a group.

DAY 3

focus
(verb) To put one's attention on something or somebody; concentrate. *Students should **focus** on their work and try to ignore the noise in the hall.*

Ask: *When I tell you to **focus** on your work, or to **focus** on me, what do I mean?* (concentrate on your work; pay attention to only you) Say: *We **focus** when we decide to look at, listen to, and think about something.* Ask students to talk about the things that draw their attention away when they are trying to **focus** on their homework. (e.g., noisy siblings; a worry) Then have students complete the Day 3 activities on page 112. You may want to do the first one as a group.

DAY 4

focus
(noun) A center of activity, interest, or attention. *Ecology will be the **focus** of our science class today.*

topic
(noun) The subject of a book, essay, or other written work. *The invention of the light bulb is the **topic** of this report.*

Say: *When we focus on something, we call the thing we have turned our attention to our **focus**. If I tell you to focus on your work, what should be your **focus**?* (work) Tell students that **topic** can be a synonym for **focus** when we are talking about a written work. Say: *You might say that the **focus** of a book is weather. Or, you could say that the book's **topic** is weather. You could also say that the **topic** is weather with a special **focus** on hurricanes.* Using textbooks, ask students for examples of **topics** and narrower **focuses** within them. Have students complete the Day 4 activities on page 112. You may want to do the first one as a group.

DAY 5

Have students complete page 113. Call on students to read aloud their answers to the writing activity.

Name_____

Day 1 address

1. How would you complete this sentence? Say it aloud to a partner.

A problem I recently had to address was _____.

2. Which sentence does not use *address* correctly? Circle your answer.

a. We need to address the traffic situation in our town.

b. You need to address the problem before it gets worse.

c. I can address after school if I am not too busy.

d. Using a dictionary will address misspellings in your writing.

3. Which sentences describe someone who *addressed* a problem or situation? Circle your answers.

a. Colleen used a magnifying glass to read the small print.

b. When the power went out, my dad found a flashlight.

c. It was snowing, but he wouldn't wear boots.

d. Jeff ignored the overdue notice for his library books.

Day 2 address

1. How would you complete this sentence? Say it aloud to a partner.

When I address a group of people, I feel _____.

2. If someone is *addressing* a crowd, what is she doing? Circle your answer.

a. writing a letter   c. counting the people

b. giving a talk   d. showing them a map

3. How might someone prepare to *address* a group? List three things someone could do to prepare.

a. _____

b. _____

c. _____

4. Who would you like to *address* your class? Why?

_____

_____

Name_____

Day 3 focus

1. How would you complete this sentence? Say it aloud to a partner.

I find it most difficult to focus in class when _____.

2. Which word is a synonym for *focus*? Circle your answer.

    a. ignore   c. concentrate

    b. attempt   d. daydream

3. Which sentence does <u>not</u> use *focus* correctly? Circle your answer.

    a. It is polite to focus on the person who is talking to you.

    b. Because Jacob focused on his book, he understood what he was reading.

    c. The cat focuses on the birds it sees in the yard.

    d. Jay was distracted and focused during class.

Day 4 focus • topic

1. How would you complete these sentences? Say them aloud to a partner.

This Saturday my focus will be _____.

I think _____ would be an interesting topic to read about.

2. Who should be the *focus* of attention for a batter in a baseball game? Circle your answer.

    a. the fans   c. the announcer

    b. the pitcher   d. the peanut seller

3. Which sentences use *topic* correctly? Circle your answers.

    a. The topic of my essay is community pride.

    b. In its topic, the newspaper announced the winner of the election.

    c. Jessie gave a speech on the topic of violence prevention.

    d. The speakers topic the issue of nutrition.

4. What was the *topic* and *focus* of a book you read recently?

topic: _____

focus: _____

Your **focus** should always be on me!

Name_____

Day 5 address • focus • topic

Fill in the bubble next to the correct answer.

1. Which sentence does not use *address* correctly?

Ⓐ Recycling is one way to address the litter problem.

Ⓑ This book addresses the issue of bullying.

Ⓒ Because she addresses, the letters get sent.

Ⓓ The plumber addressed the situation of the leaky pipe.

2. Which sentence describes someone who is *addressing* people?

Ⓕ The senator adjusts his microphone as he speaks.

Ⓖ The student carefully writes her name at the top of the paper.

Ⓗ In the library, Jerry sits quietly with his classmates.

Ⓙ Lindsay makes a note of the next assignment.

3. Which statement would not be true if you were the *focus* of attention in class?

Ⓐ Everyone in the room would listen to you.

Ⓑ You would see people looking at you.

Ⓒ Nobody would notice if you left the room.

Ⓓ The teacher would hear what you said.

4. Which of these might be a good *topic* for a report in history class?

Ⓕ how to build a treehouse

Ⓖ the discovery of trade routes to India

Ⓗ chemistry experiments

Ⓙ skateboard safety

Writing   Write about what you do to help yourself *focus* on your schoolwork. Use at least one of this week's words in your writing.

_____

_____

_____

_____

CUMULATIVE REVIEW
WORDS FROM WEEKS 19–26

accuracy
accurate
address
aspect
condition
critical
criticism
critique
dominant
emphasis
emphasize
factor
focus
imitate
imitation
insignificant
modification
modify
pattern
precise
precision
prevalent
primary
significance
significant
substitute
topic

Days 1–4

Each day's activity is a cloze paragraph that students complete with words or forms of words that they have learned in weeks 19–26. Before students begin, pronounce each word in the box on the student page, have students repeat each word, and then review each word's meaning(s). **Other ways to review the words:**

- Start a sentence containing one of the words and have students finish the sentence orally. For example:

  *I'd like your **criticism** of…*
  *I am worried about the **condition** of…*

- Provide students with a definition and ask them to supply the word that fits it.

- Ask questions that require students to know the meaning of each word. For example:

  *What helps you maintain your **focus** in school?*
  *How might you **modify** the school year?*

- Have students use each word in a sentence.

Day 5

Start by reviewing the eight words not practiced on Days 1–4: **condition**, **criticism**, **critique**, **focus**, **imitate**, **modification**, **pattern**, **precise**. Write the words on the board and have students repeat them after you. Provide a sentence for one of the words. Ask students to think of their own sentence and share it with a partner. Call on several students to share their sentences. Follow the same procedure with the remaining words. Then have students complete the code-breaker activity.

Extension Ideas

Use any of the following activities to help integrate the vocabulary words into other content areas:

- Have students **imitate** the style of a famous poem. Encourage them to **pattern** their own poem after the author's.

- Have students suggest a **modification** to a fairy tale. They can write their new tales and **critique** each other's work.

- Have students discuss the importance of being **precise** in science. Choose an experiment to conduct with the students to illustrate this point.

| accuracy | critical | imitation | prevalent | significance |
| address | dominant | insignificant | primary | substitute |

Day 1

Fill in the blanks with words from the word box.

Coral snakes are _____ from the southern United States

to South America. Their main _____ is that they are very

poisonous. Coral snakes are very exact when they strike. They bite lizards, smaller

snakes, and rodents with great _____. They aren't naturally

aggressive, but their bite is serious for humans. It's a _____

emergency! Other snakes copy the coral snake's red, yellow, and black bands. This

_____ makes predators believe the other snakes are poisonous,

too. Poisonous or not, treat all snakes with respect and keep your distance!

Day 2

Fill in the blanks with words from the word box.

In some countries, there are very few trees to use for buildings. In these places,

the amount of lumber used for buildings is _____. How do people

_____ the challenge of building a home? Their _____

for wood is adobe, or bricks made of sand, clay, and straw. Adobe is one of the oldest

and most _____ kinds of building material in the world. Also, adobe

keeps the inside of buildings so cool that in hot climates it is the _____,

or main, method of construction.

Daily Academic Vocabulary

accurate	emphasis	emphasize	precision	topic
aspects	factor	modified	significant	

Day 3

Fill in the blanks with words from the word box.

I read an interesting article last week. Its _____ was the

importance of flamenco. Flamenco is a _____ form of folk music

and dance in Spanish culture. Its many _____, or characteristics,

include singing, dancing, and guitar playing. Special attention is often given to its

dancers, but in traditional flamenco, the _____ is on the song. The

songs are often poems full of emotion. Dancers begin to dance when they *feel* the

music. The music and dancing is not exact, but many people believe flamenco's

beauty is in its feeling and lack of _____.

Day 4

Fill in the blanks with words from the word box.

Books on natural disasters often _____ hurricanes. One

_____ that makes hurricanes so dangerous is the difficulty of

predicting their paths. Luckily, more _____ predictions are resulting

from newer technology. Scientists can now track hurricanes with satellites. They also

use airplanes that have been _____ by adding special equipment.

Pilots fly these airplanes right into the center of a hurricane! The information they

gather is used to warn the public. Those brave pilots should certainly be thanked!

Crack the Code!

Write one of the words from the word box on the lines next to each clue.

accuracy	criticism	focus	pattern	significant
accurate	critique	imitate	precise	substitute
address	dominant	imitation	precision	topic
aspect	emphasis	insignificant	prevalent	
condition	emphasize	modification	primary	
critical	factor	modify	significance	

1. the general state of someone or something __ __ __ __ __ __ __ __ __
            1

2. to copy the actions of someone __ __ __ __ __ __ __
        2

3. the act of judging good and bad __ __ __ __ __ __ __ __ __
        3

4. to concentrate on something __ __ __ __ __
        4

5. to say what is good or bad about something __ __ __ __ __ __ __ __
        5

6. to act following a model __ __ __ __ __ __ __
        6

7. very accurate __ __ __ __ __ __ __
        7

8. found or happening frequently __ __ __ __ __ __ __ __ __
        8

Now use the numbers under the letters to crack the code. Write the letters on the lines below. The words will complete this sentence:

A scientist who studies snakes is a _____.

h __ __ __ __ __ __ __ g __ __ __
7 5 6 7 3 1 8 1   2 4 3

Daily Academic Vocabulary

associate • association
relationship • relative to

Use the reproducible definitions on page 184 and the suggestions on page 6 to introduce the words for each day.

DAY 1

associate
(verb) To connect with something else in your mind. *I always **associate** roses with my mother's birthday.*

Say: *A special smell often makes us think of something else, something we **associate** with that smell because of our experience.* Offer a personal example. Then ask: *What is a smell that you **associate** with something else?* Then offer an example that does not involve smell. You might say: *Maybe you **associate** cats with your uncle because he has five cats.* Ask students for more examples. Point out that we usually use the verb **associate** with the preposition "with." Then have students complete the Day 1 activities on page 119. You may want to do the first one as a group.

DAY 2

association
(noun) The connection of one feeling, thought, or emotion with another. *I have a strong **association** between lemonade and hot summer days.*

Say: *When we associate, we make a connection—an **association**.* Give an example of one of your own **associations**. (e.g., a song and an event; a food and a place) Ask: *What are some **associations** that you have?* Then have students complete the Day 2 activities on page 119. You may want to do the first one as a group.

DAY 3

relationship
(noun) The way in which things are connected. *After the Revolutionary War, the **relationship** between Britain and America changed.*

Say: *You have a **relationship** with a friend and a **relationship** with your parents. You are connected to those people in different ways. We also talk about **relationships** between things, ideas, or events.* Ask: *How can two ideas or events have a **relationship**?* (e.g., one can cause the other; they can have similar aspects or results) After responses, ask: *What is the **relationship** between sunlight and plant growth? What are other events or ideas we've studied that have a **relationship**?* Then have students complete the Day 3 activities on page 120. You may want to do the first one as a group.

DAY 4

relative to
(adj. phrase) Compared to. ***Relative to** my interest in sports, my interest in computers is high.*

Ask: *Is our school big or is it small? It is difficult to answer that question unless we think about our school as it is **relative to**—or compared to—another school. It may be big **relative to** the old one-room schoolhouse, but is it big **relative to** other schools you know about?* Open the question to discussion. Then have students complete the Day 4 activities on page 120. You may want to do the first one as a group.

DAY 5

Have students complete page 121. Call on students to read aloud their answers to the writing activity.

Name_____

Day 1 associate

1. How would you complete this sentence? Say it aloud to a partner.

I associate _____ with _____.

2. Which word is a synonym for *associate?* Circle your answer.

a. conduct   c. connect

b. separate   d. avoid

3. In which sentences is *associate* used correctly? Circle your answers.

a. The children associate pirates with treasure maps and parrots.

b. Sara associates her sneezes because of blooming flowers.

c. I wonder if Columbus associated the smell of the sea with adventure.

d. What do you associate in deep-sea diving?

4. What do you *associate* with starting a new school year?

_____

_____

Day 2 association

1. How would you complete this sentence? Say it aloud to a partner.

I make a pleasant association between _____ and _____.

2. Which sentence describes someone making an *association?* Circle your answer.

a. Brendan forgets to take his flute to band practice.

b. When Claire hears that song, she thinks of her aunt's farm.

c. At the last minute, Susan remembers to buy a birthday card.

d. My father promises to take me to the golf course on Saturday.

3. In which sentence could *association* fill in the blank? Circle your answer.

a. I think we are going in the wrong _____.

b. The gracious hosts showed an _____ for their guests by offering tea.

c. His _____ in the proper way to hold the bat was helpful to the new player.

d. My dog makes an _____ between the car and the veterinarian.

Name_____

Day 3 relationship

1. How would you complete this sentence? Say it aloud to a partner.

I think that having a good relationship with a friend means _____.

2. In which sentences is *relationship* used correctly? Circle your answers.

    a. The kings and queens of Europe were often relationships.

    b. Dancers see a relationship between music and movement.

    c. My great-grandmother is a relationship.

    d. Doctors know that there is a relationship between health and diet.

3. In which sentences could the underlined word be replaced with *relationship*? Circle your answers.

    a. Because my guitar teacher and I have a good <u>connection</u>, I enjoy my lessons.

    b. The country's people have long suffered under a <u>dictatorship</u>.

    c. The <u>conversation</u> between the scientists was about developing alternative fuels.

    d. We studied the <u>tie</u> between air pollution and breathing problems.

4. What is the *relationship* between plants and sunlight?

_____

_____

Day 4 relative to

1. How would you complete this sentence? Say it aloud to a partner.

Relative to _____, I find _____ easy.

2. Which sentences use *relative to* correctly? Circle your answers.

    a. This device is used to relative to flow the fuel to the engine.

    b. The music contest judges consider the performance of one singer relative to another.

    c. Relative to the early flight suits, the ones the astronauts wear today are comfortable.

    d. In relative to, it is difficult to make a decision.

3. You are asked to discuss the merits of one book *relative to* the merits of another. What are you to do? Circle your answer.

    a. compare the books to each other   c. find the books in the library

    b. reread the books   d. recommend the books to a friend

Daily Academic Vocabulary

| **Day 5** | **associate • association**
relationship • relative to |

Fill in the bubble next to the correct answer.

1. Which sentence does <u>not</u> use *associate* correctly?

Ⓐ My cat associates the sound of the can opener with his dinner.

Ⓑ I have learned to associate serious study with good test scores.

Ⓒ The farmers associate the failure of the crop with the bad weather.

Ⓓ I can see no associate between the reading and the questions.

2. Which sentence describes someone making an *association*?

Ⓕ When James saw the yellow pencil, he thought of the first day of school.

Ⓖ Peggy filled out the application carefully, hoping for good results.

Ⓗ Because he was tired, the explorer forgot to pack his compass.

Ⓙ The teacher carefully considered her response to the student's question.

3. To which question below would *relationship* be the correct answer?

Ⓐ What word do we use to talk about the movement of the planets?

Ⓑ What word do we use to talk about the way things are connected?

Ⓒ What word names how little children learn to talk?

Ⓓ What do you call the brother of your mother or father?

4. In which sentence is *relative to* used correctly?

Ⓕ Conner relatives to so much that he cannot find the correct answer.

Ⓖ I certainly could relative to my work on the project to the weekend.

Ⓗ In relative to the sun is our nearest star.

Ⓙ Relative to the average 12-year-old, Kim is an exceptional pitcher.

Writing Write about the smells, the sounds, and the sights you *associate* with your favorite season of the year. Be sure to use at least one of this week's words in your writing.

_____

_____

_____

_____

WEEK 29

constant • consistent
consistency

Use the reproducible definitions on page 185 and the suggestions on page 6 to introduce the words for each day.

DAY 1

constant
(adj.) Going on without stopping; not changing. *The constant sound of lapping waves soothed me to sleep.*

Tell students that when something is **constant** it does not stop and start again, but starts and does not stop. Say: *If your stomach hurts all day, the pain is constant. The Earth's revolving is constant. It never stops.* Then say: *Things that don't change are also constant. If the temperature of a room doesn't change, we say it is at a constant temperature.* Ask: *What else can be constant?* Then have students complete the Day 1 activities on page 123. You may want to do the first one as a group.

DAY 2

consistent
(adj.) Always behaving the same way or having the same ideas. *Because the teacher is consistent in his expectations, the students know what to do.*

Say: *We say someone is consistent in their behavior or in their thinking when they always act or think the same way.* Ask students why it might be easier to be with someone who is **consistent**. (e.g., predictable; can be counted on) Then ask: *If I ask you to make sure to keep a consistent verb tense in your writing, what do I mean? If you head or label your papers in a consistent manner, what do you do?* Then have students complete the Day 2 activities on page 123. You may want to do the first one as a group.

DAY 3

consistency
(noun) The act of behaving the same way or having the same ideas. *His consistency on the field led his teammates to count on his winning plays.*

Say: *When someone is consistent, we say that he or she acts with consistency.* Then ask: *Where do you see consistency in school?* Ask students whether they think **consistency** is always a good thing. *In what areas or places might consistency not be a good thing?* Encourage students to use the word **consistency** in their responses. Then have students complete the Day 3 activities on page 124. You may want to do the first one as a group.

DAY 4

consistency
(noun) The thickness, stiffness, or firmness of something; texture. *The consistency of the glue was too thin, so the cardboard pieces just slipped off each other.*

Say: *We often hear people talk about the consistency of food.* Ask: *What might someone mean who says, "I like the taste of this pudding, but not its consistency?"* (e.g., too lumpy; too sticky; bad texture) *What is the difference in consistency between oatmeal and chocolate milk?* Then have students complete the Day 4 activities on page 124. You may want to do the first one as a group.

DAY 5

Have students complete page 125. Call on students to read aloud their answers to the writing activity.

Name _____

Day 1 constant

1. How would you complete this sentence? Say it aloud to a partner.

I wish I had a constant supply of _____.

2. Which sentences describe something that is *constant*? Circle your answers.

    a. The sound of traffic is the ever-present background noise in our lives.

    b. The school bell rings at the beginning and at the end of the day.

    c. It often rains during the spring in that part of the world.

    d. In the computer lab, the low hum of the machines goes on day and night.

3. In which sentence could the underlined word be replaced with *constant*? Circle your answer.

    a. In his <u>concluding</u> paragraph, the writer summarized his points.

    b. The final <u>consonant</u> of the word must be clearly pronounced.

    c. Prices in the market are <u>unpredictable</u> from day to day.

    d. The safest drivers maintain a <u>steady</u> speed on the highway.

4. List three things that are *constant*.

    a. _____

    b. _____

    c. _____

Day 2 consistent

1. How would you complete this sentence? Say it aloud to a partner.

I think it is important to be consistent in _____.

2. Which sentence uses *consistent* correctly? Circle your answer.

    a. The zookeeper can predict when the lion will eat because the animal is consistent.

    b. The politician wants to know what I think because I am a consistent.

    c. That consistent has won the competition by performing exceptionally well.

    d. Because the weather is consistent, I don't know what to wear.

3. Which of these actions is *consistent*? Circle your answer.

    a. Sometimes the band will play for the school.

    b. Classes often form kickball teams.

    c. The lunchroom serves a different meal each day.

    d. At the same time each morning, the teachers take attendance.

Day 3 | consistency

1. How would you complete this sentence? Say it aloud to a partner.

Consistency in _____ can help a student by _____.

2. Which phrase best completes this sentence? Circle your answer.

When someone behaves with consistency, we can _____.

    a. forget to invite him to the party
    b. never know what she'll do next
    c. assume that he won't know the answer
    d. predict how she will react in a situation

3. Which sentences use *consistency* correctly? Circle your answers.

    a. I consistency change my mind about what I want to do when I grow up.
    b. It is hard to predict what he will do because there is no consistency in his actions.
    c. The identical results of the experiment show consistency.
    d. The noise from the storm is heard consistency throughout the house.

Day 4 | consistency

1. How would you complete this sentence? Say it aloud to a partner.

I don't like to eat _____ because it has a strange consistency.

2. Which of these words does <u>not</u> describe a *consistency*? Circle your answer.

    a. thickness   c. firmness
    b. sweetness   d. stiffness

3. Which word or phrase would best complete this sentence? Circle your answer.

The worker tested the consistency of the _____.

    a. jackhammer   c. wet cement
    b. nails   d. screws and bolts

4. Name something that can be described by each *consistency*.

    a. thick   _____

    b. lumpy _____

    c. runny _____

    d. sticky _____

> This stew has a chunky **consistency**.

Name_____

Day 5 constant • consistent • consistency

Fill in the bubble next to the correct answer.

1. Which phrase best completes this sentence?

Constant noise is disturbing because it _____.

Ⓐ is out of tune

Ⓑ is too loud

Ⓒ goes on without stopping

Ⓓ can't be clearly heard

2. Which sentence does not use *consistent* correctly?

Ⓕ The surgeon's consistent choice of music is classical.

Ⓖ The little children consistent ask for help with their reading.

Ⓗ Be consistent in your commands when you train your dog.

Ⓙ The consistent weather in southern Florida is warm and sunny.

3. Which sentence does not describe someone who acts or thinks with *consistency*?

Ⓐ I don't know what kind of music my sister will listen to next.

Ⓑ I know what my dad will say before I ask because he never changes his mind.

Ⓒ Jennifer always tests the water temperature with her toe before jumping in.

Ⓓ I sit down every day at 4 o'clock to begin my homework.

4. How might a chef test the *consistency* of bread dough?

Ⓕ She would feel it to see if it was warm enough.

Ⓖ He would taste it to see if it was too salty.

Ⓗ She would look to see if it was the right color.

Ⓙ He would roll it in his hands to see if it was firm enough.

Writing   Write about something that you do with *consistency*. Use at least one of this week's words in your writing.

_____

_____

_____

_____

conform • correspond
corresponding • correspondence

Use the reproducible definitions on page 186 and the suggestions on page 6 to introduce the words for each day.

DAY 1

conform
(verb) To act in a way that agrees with a rule or standard. *His shirt must* **conform** *to the school dress code.*

Say: *When we* **conform**, *we do what someone or something else says. When you obey our class rules, you* **conform** *to those rules. When you choose to dress like other kids, you* **conform**. Ask: *What would I mean if I told you your report does not* **conform** *to the directions of the assignment? If I said the results of the experiment* **conformed** *to our prediction?* Then have students complete the Day 1 activities on page 127. You may want to do the first one as a group.

DAY 2

correspond
(verb) To be in agreement with or match something. *The birds I see in that nest* **correspond** *to the ones pictured in this book.*

Ask one student to summarize what you have done in class today. Ask another student the same question. Then ask the class: *Does (student's name)'s summary* **correspond** *to, or match, (other student's name)'s summary? What do I mean if I say, "The character's actions don't* **correspond** *to what he says"?* Then have students complete the Day 2 activities on page 127. You may want to do the first one as a group.

DAY 3

corresponding
(adj.) In agreement or matching with. *Fill in the bubble with the* **corresponding** *letter of your answer.*

Invite several students to come up to the board. Trace their hands. Have the students stand next to the outline of their hand. Tell the class: *These students are standing next to* **corresponding** *outlines of their hands. Their hand and their outline go together.* Then ask: *If a test gives you a word and asks that you find the* **corresponding** *definition in a list, what are you supposed to do?* (Find the definition that goes with the word.) Then have students complete the Day 3 activities on page 128. You may want to do the first one as a group.

DAY 4

correspond
(verb) To write to another person. *I* **correspond** *with my grandmother who lives in Brazil.*

correspondence
(noun) Communication in writing. **Correspondence** *by letters is no longer practiced by most people.*

Say: *To* **correspond** *with someone means to communicate in writing. The act of exchanging written messages is called the* **correspondence**. Ask: *Have you ever* **corresponded** *with anyone? Who? How did you* **correspond**? Discuss the difference between sending letters and e-mailing or instant messaging. Then have students complete the Day 4 activities on page 128. You may want to do the first one as a group.

DAY 5

Have students complete page 129. Call on students to read aloud their answers to the writing activity.

Name_____

Day 1 conform

1. **How would you complete this sentence? Say it aloud to a partner.**

   One thing I conform to is _____.

2. **How would you *conform* to standards of behavior? Circle your answer.**

   a. do whatever you want to do
   b. make sure your clothing matches with someone
   c. do what everyone else does
   d. follow your own rules

3. **In which of these sentences does someone *conform*? Circle your answers.**

   a. Sharif followed his teacher's directions for the project.
   b. Anna went to the movie by herself.
   c. Aisha and her mother had a conference with her teacher.
   d. Kareem made his friendly letter look like the example in the book.

Day 2 correspond

1. **How would you complete this sentence? Say it aloud to a partner.**

   My interests correspond with _____.

2. **Which description *corresponds* with the word "parrot"? Circle your answer.**

   a. a four-legged animal with rough fur
   b. a fruit with yellow skin and sweet flesh
   c. a tropical bird with colorful feathers
   d. a reptile with a long tongue

3. **Which sentences use *correspond* correctly? Circle your answers.**

   a. The correspond reported from the scene of the action.
   b. Be sure that your spelling corresponds with the spelling in the dictionary.
   c. Teamwork requires good correspond.
   d. We enjoy the same concerts because our tastes in music correspond.

4. **Which shape name *corresponds* to which shape? Label each picture.**

   oval   circle   rectangle   square

_____   _____   _____   _____

Name_____

Day 3 corresponding

1. How would you complete this sentence? Say it aloud to a partner.

When I meet a new person, I look for corresponding interests such as _____.

2. In which sentence is *corresponding* used correctly? Circle your answer.

   a. The student matches the Roman numeral "III" to the corresponding number "3."
   b. The corresponding will not cooperate with the authorities.
   c. I think that this word is the corresponding.
   d. The music is corresponding to the cheering crowd.

3. Every car has a steering wheel. What is the *corresponding* part of a bicycle? Circle your answer.

   a. tires
   b. hand breaks
   c. handlebars
   d. seat

Day 4 correspond • correspondence

1. How would you complete these sentences? Say them aloud to a partner.

I wish I could correspond with _____.

A correspondence between _____ and _____ would be interesting to read.

2. List three pieces of information you would write if you were to *correspond* with someone in another country.

   a. _____

   b. _____

   c. _____

3. In which sentence is *correspondence* <u>not</u> used correctly? Circle your answer.

   a. The correspondence between my grandmother and her sister went on for decades.
   b. In their correspondence, Carol and John talked about their fears and hopes.
   c. Some people like to use special paper for their correspondence.
   d. The campers correspondence with their friends at home.

Name_____

conform • correspond
corresponding • correspondence

Daily Academic Vocabulary

Fill in the bubble next to the correct answer.

1. Which phrase completes the following sentence?

When someone conforms, he or she does <u>not</u> _____.

Ⓐ follow the rules

Ⓑ do what others do

Ⓒ behave according to a standard

Ⓓ act independently

> I correspond with my brother in South America.

2. In which sentence is *correspond* <u>not</u> used correctly?

Ⓕ I will correspond with my sister at college.

Ⓖ My answers correspond with the ones in the book.

Ⓗ Your correspond to this question is not correct.

Ⓙ That advice corresponds with what my mother said.

3. In which sentence could *corresponding* fill in the blank?

Ⓐ The _____ was published in a book.

Ⓑ Write the vocabulary word, and then study the _____ definition.

Ⓒ The candidates for mayor engage in a _____ tonight.

Ⓓ The _____ sang well in the concert hall last Saturday.

4. Which sentence does <u>not</u> describe someone taking part in a *correspondence* with someone else?

Ⓕ Rachel searched for a stamp to put on her letter.

Ⓖ The girl eagerly awaited the letter from her friend.

Ⓗ Steven chatted on his cellphone.

Ⓙ George Washington used a quill pen when he wrote to Martha.

Writing Write what you might include in a letter if you *corresponded* with someone famous. Use at least one of this week's words in your writing.

_____

_____

_____

distinct • distinction
differentiate • discriminate

Use the reproducible definitions on page 187 and the suggestions on page 6 to introduce the words for each day.

DAY 1

distinct
(adj.) Clearly different from someone or something else. *This puppy's distinct markings separate it from the others in the litter.*

Say: *When we use distinct, we mean that something stands out.* Ask: *What do you think is a distinct feature of our town or your neighborhood? What would stand out to a visitor?* Students might mention natural features or unusual buildings. Encourage students to use the word distinct in their responses. Then have students complete the Day 1 activities on page 131. You may want to do the first one as a group.

DAY 2

distinction
(noun) A feature or mark that makes someone or something different from another. *There is an important distinction between scanning a story and reading it closely.*

Write the word on the board and underline the adjective within it. ("distinct") Tell students that the thing that makes a thing or person distinct from others is a **distinction.** Ask: *What is a distinction between social studies and math?* (e.g., more reading in one; more numbers in another) Have students complete the Day 2 activities on page 131. You may want to do the first one as a group.

DAY 3

differentiate
(verb) To find or see differences or distinctions between things. *I can differentiate between a cube and a square.*

Say: *We differentiate when we see the differences between things. For instance, how can we differentiate between a shark and a dolphin?* (e.g., fish versus mammal; fins) *What differentiates our classroom from a first-grade classroom?* Encourage students to use the word **differentiate** in their responses. Then have students complete the Day 3 activities on page 132. You may want to do the first one as a group.

DAY 4

discriminate
(verb) To see a clear difference; to make a distinction. *With her telescope, she can discriminate between the two planets.*

Say: *"Differentiate" and discriminate are synonyms. Although you may know a different definition of discriminate, it is also used to mean "to see a difference." In science, for instance, you might be asked if you can discriminate between a healthy plant and a dead plant. How would you do that?* (look for differences between a healthy and a dead plant) *What would you do if you wanted to discriminate between instrument sounds in a piece of music?* (listen for differences; listen for what is distinct) Have students complete the Day 4 activities on page 132. You may want to do the first one as a group.

DAY 5

Have students complete page 133. Call on students to read aloud their answers to the writing activity.

Daily Academic Vocabulary

Day 1 distinct

1. How would you complete this sentence? Say it aloud to a partner.

My _____ makes me distinct from the rest of my family.

2. Which word is a synonym for *distinct*? Circle your answer.

a. different
b. difficult
c. terrible
d. positive

3. In which sentence is *distinct* used correctly? Circle your answer.

a. I cannot distinct one character from another in this book.
b. You should note that this question is distinct from the others on the test.
c. The distinct from the chemistry lab filled the entire building.
d. He improved after practicing his distinct.

4. What makes your classroom *distinct*?

_____

_____

Day 2 distinction

1. How would you complete this sentence? Say it aloud to a partner.

One distinction between elementary school and high school is _____.

2. You have noticed a *distinction* between one flag and another. What have you noticed? Circle your answer.

a. Both flags are the same size.
b. One flag is exactly the same shape as the other.
c. One flag has a leaf and one has a circle.
d. The colors on the flags are very bright.

3. Which sentence uses *distinction* correctly? Circle your answer.

a. The distinction was just like all of the rest of them.
b. The president is in the distinction to increase the company's profits.
c. Distinctions on this television show are not interesting.
d. Notice the distinction in color between the adult and the baby birds.

Day 3 differentiate

1. How would you complete this sentence? Say it aloud to a partner.

It is easy to differentiate my _____ from my friends'.

2. What do you look for when you *differentiate*? Circle your answers.

a. differences
b. similarities
c. distinctions
d. comparisons

3. List two ways you can *differentiate* a strong paragraph from a weak paragraph.

a. _____

b. _____

Day 4 discriminate

1. How would you complete this sentence? Say it aloud to a partner.

I can discriminate between a _____ and a _____.

2. Which sentence does <u>not</u> use *discriminate* correctly? Circle your answer.

a. Maria will choose her discriminate flower.
b. Because he is colorblind, Gus is unable to discriminate colors.
c. Jamila is unable to discriminate among the choices.
d. In his experiment, Peter will attempt to discriminate between gold and lead.

3. How can you *discriminate* between a square and a rectangle?

_____

_____

4. How do you *discriminate* among characters in a book or story?

_____

_____

Name_____

Fill in the bubble next to the correct answer.

1. You are asked to write about what makes whales *distinct* from other ocean creatures. What do you write about?

   Ⓐ their ability to live underwater

   Ⓑ their enormous size

   Ⓒ their diet of fish

   Ⓓ their color

2. Which sentence uses *distinction* correctly?

   Ⓕ I cannot distinction between the leopard and the cheetah.

   Ⓖ Having a quiz tomorrow is a distinction possibility.

   Ⓗ There is a distinction between the African elephant and the Asian elephant.

   Ⓙ He does not have the ability to distinction between the players.

3. Which sentence does <u>not</u> use *differentiate* correctly?

   Ⓐ Can you differentiate between the two countries?

   Ⓑ The science experiment attempted to differentiate various molds.

   Ⓒ Tim can differentiate between various types of music.

   Ⓓ Carlos determined the differentiate between fruits and vegetables.

4. When you *discriminate,* what do you do?

   Ⓕ look between things

   Ⓖ look for similarities

   Ⓗ look for differences

   Ⓙ look for problems

Writing Write about your family's *distinct* characteristics. Use at least one of this week's words in your writing.

_____

_____

_____

_____

represent • representative
symbolize • symbol • symbolic

Use the reproducible definitions on page 188 and the suggestions on page 6 to introduce the words for each day.

DAY 1

represent
(verb) To stand for or be a sign of something. *The blue ribbons I won at the state fair represent much hard work.*

representative
(adj.) Being an example of a group or kind. *Chandler showed the class a representative sample of his seashell collection.*

Tell students that something might **represent** one idea to one person and another idea to someone else. Say: *To you, blooming flowers might represent spring and sunshine, but to your friend, the same flowers might represent sneezing and watery eyes.* Ask: *What do flowers represent to you?* Then introduce the adjective form by asking: *If you were to choose one flower to be representative of flowers, what would you choose? Why?* Students may use the sentence starter, "___ is **representative** of flowers because ___." Then have students complete the Day 1 activities on page 135. You may want to do the first one as a group.

DAY 2

representative
(noun) A person or a thing that is typical of a group. *The visitors to the zoo watched the snake, a representative of the reptile family.*

Say: *When we choose a typical member of a group to represent the entire group, that member is a representative.* Ask: *What animal would you choose as a representative of mammals? As a representative of birds? As a representative of fish?* Then have students complete the Day 2 activities on page 135. You may want to do the first one as a group.

DAY 3

symbolize
(verb) To stand for or represent something else. *In this story, the kites symbolize the free spirits of the people.*

Say: *Often, authors and artists use something to symbolize an idea or feeling. Words, objects, colors, and even sounds can symbolize something else.* Ask: *What colors or objects could an artist use to symbolize sadness? What could an owl symbolize in a story?* Then have students complete the Day 3 activities on page 136. You may want to do the first one as a group.

DAY 4

symbol
(noun) Something that stands for or represents something else. *The olive branch is a symbol of peace.*

symbolic
(adj.) Acting as a symbol. *The handshake is a symbolic gesture of goodwill.*

Say: *We use symbols every day. Think about street signs and traffic lights. What is a symbol for "stop"? For "go"?* Write the noun on the board, and then add "-ic." Tell students that the ending turns the noun into an adjective. Say: *Symbols are often used in books and stories.* Recall a story or book the class has read with a **symbol**. (e.g., the sled in Lois Lowry's *The Giver*) Ask: *What was symbolic about the (symbol in the story)? What did it represent?* Say: *Many things around us are symbolic. What images are symbolic on our country's flag? What do they stand for?* Then have students complete the Day 4 activities on page 136. You may want to complete the first one as a group.

DAY 5

Have students complete page 137. Call on students to read aloud their answers to the writing activity.

Daily Academic Vocabulary

Day 1 **represent • representative**

1. How would you complete these sentences? Say them aloud to a partner.

My _____ represents _____ to me.

I think that _____ is representative of the best shows on television.

2. In which sentence could *represent* replace the underlined words? Circle your answer.

   a. The instructions tell us what to do <u>in case of</u> an emergency.

   b. On the poster I made, the trees <u>stand for</u> the importance of nature.

   c. I <u>identify with</u> the main character in the story because I have the same problem.

   d. The committee members <u>are concerned about</u> the safety of our streets.

3. Which sentence uses *representative* correctly? Circle your answer.

   a. I have voiced my unusual and representative opinion.

   b. Chicago is representative because it is unlike any other city.

   c. Corn representatives a vegetable that must be grown on a farm or in a garden.

   d. Tyler is representative of a good athlete because he is strong and dedicated.

4. What do these signs *represent*? Label each sign.

$$+ \qquad\qquad X \qquad\qquad \div \qquad\qquad =$$

_____   _____   _____   _____

Day 2 **representative**

1. How would you complete this sentence? Say it aloud to a partner.

I think that _____ is a representative of heroes because _____.

2. In which sentence could *representative* fill in the blank? Circle your answer.

   a. The artists _____ the subjects of their paintings in different ways.

   b. We studied the black widow spider as a _____ of poisonous spiders.

   c. Jill talks _____ to her teachers and to her fellow students in the class.

   d. The students were directed to put the papers in the proper _____.

3. Which phrase could replace *representative* in this sentence? Circle your answer.

This rock serves as a representative of the kind of rock found in our area.

   a. typical example   c. strange example

   b. rare sample   d. modern sample

Daily Academic Vocabulary

Day 3 **symbolize**

1. How would you complete this sentence? Say it aloud to a partner.

I think that a light could be used in a story to symbolize _____ because _____.

2. Which of these words is a synonym for *symbolize*? Circle your answer.

a. disagree   c. decide

b. compromise   d. represent

3. Which sentences use *symbolize* correctly? Circle your answers.

a. The Statue of Liberty symbolized hope and freedom to new immigrants.

b. The viewers did not symbolize the man in the portrait.

c. The hourglass in the painting symbolizes the passing of time.

d. The symbolize of Smokey the Bear is known around the world.

Day 4 **symbol • symbolic**

1. How would you complete these sentences? Say them aloud to a partner.

If I were drawing a picture, I would draw a _____ as a symbol for happiness.

I think a _____ is a symbolic gesture of friendship.

2. Write the letter of each landform next to the *symbolic* image you might find for it on a map.

a. mountain   ___ 🌲🌲🌲

b. forest   ___ ⌄

c. desert   ___ ⛰️

                  🌵

d. valley   ___

3. List or draw three *symbols* that you know.

a. _____

b. _____

c. _____

*What would be a good **symbol** for a parrot?*

Name_____

Day 5 | **represent • representative**
symbolize • symbol • symbolic

Fill in the bubble next to the correct answer.

1. Which sentence does <u>not</u> use *represent* correctly?

Ⓐ The letter on my brother's jacket represents his athletic achievements.

Ⓑ I sent flowers to my mother to represent my love for her.

Ⓒ This ring is represent of my friendship with Anna.

Ⓓ The blue lines on the map represent rivers.

2. If you are studying a *representative* string instrument, which of these are you studying?

Ⓕ drums

Ⓖ saxophone

Ⓗ trumpet

Ⓙ violin

3. In which sentence could *symbolize* fill in the blank?

Ⓐ The lightning bolts on the weather map _____ thunderstorms.

Ⓑ The farmer used a tractor to _____ his field.

Ⓒ The _____ in that book confused me.

Ⓓ I _____ by reading the list over and over.

4. In which sentence is *symbol* used correctly?

Ⓕ This rooster symbols morning.

Ⓖ The photograph is a symbol of my friend and me on the roller coaster.

Ⓗ A ship's anchor is a symbol for the navy.

Ⓙ The scary movie made me symbol.

Writing If you were writing a story and wanted to use a *symbol* to stand for time, what would it be? What would be *symbolic* of time? Use at least two of this week's words in your writing.

_____

_____

_____

_____

determine • influence

Use the reproducible definitions on page 189 and the suggestions on page 6 to introduce the words for each day.

DAY 1

determine
(verb) To decide or settle an issue or matter. *The election will **determine** our representative on the student council.*

Say: *When we **determine** something, we decide or settle it. When I decide what assignment to give you for homework, I **determine** what your homework will be.* Then say: *Let's imagine that you have a class project that involves constructing something. Can you think of some sentences using **determine** that describe the steps you will take?* (e.g., **determine** what the project will be; **determine** what materials are needed; **determine** a schedule) Then have students complete the Day 1 activities on page 139. You might want to do the first one as a group.

DAY 2

determine
(verb) To find out by watching and checking; to discover. *Doctors **determine** how well the medicine is working by examining the patients.*

Say: *We often find this use of **determine** in science and social studies. We might read, for example, that scientists used new technology to **determine** the age of dinosaur bones, or that the settlers **determined** that the soil was not rich enough to grow healthy crops.* Then ask: *How can you **determine** what your homework is for tonight?* Then have students complete the Day 2 activities on page 139. You might want to do the first one as a group.

DAY 3

determine
(verb) To bring about; to be the cause of. *The amount of light and water will **determine** how well the plant grows.*

Ask: *Have you ever heard it said that the choices you make today **determine** your future? What aspects of life might this be true for?* (e.g., health habits; how much effort you put into school or hobbies) Then ask: *What **determines** the grade you get on an assignment?* Then have students complete the Day 3 activities on page 140. You may want to do the first one as a group.

DAY 4

influence
(verb) To have an effect on someone or something. *The behavior of older children **influences** younger children.*

(noun) The effect of someone or something. *Researchers are studying the **influence** of air pollution on our health.*

Say: *Someone or something might **influence**, or make a difference in, our behavior or our thinking. I try to **influence** your learning by teaching you.* Ask: *Who has **influenced** you in a positive way?* Then say: *The way someone or something **influences** a person or a thing is called an **influence**.* Ask: *Who or what has been an **influence** in your learning? On your decisions?* Encourage students to use the word **influence** in their responses. Then have students complete the Day 4 activities on page 140. You may want to do the first one as a group.

DAY 5

Have students complete page 141. Call on students to read aloud their answers to the writing activity.

Name_____

Day 1 determine

1. **How would you complete this sentence? Say it aloud to a partner.**

   My parents allow me to determine _____.

2. **Which sentences use *determine* correctly? Circle your answers.**

   a. After much discussion, we determined to call our team The Tigercats.
   b. During the gold rush, this creek was determined for the precious metal.
   c. We will determine which route to take by studying the map.
   d. The unreliable quarterback is a determine to the team.

3. **In which sentence could *determined* replace the underlined word or words? Circle your answer.**

   a. I couldn't get my dog to <u>settle down</u> after we played ball.
   b. Mrs. Jones <u>discovered</u> a mouse in her closet.
   c. The boys <u>made a choice</u> between the two flavors of ice cream.
   d. The principal <u>decided</u> where each class would sit in the cafeteria.

Day 2 determine

1. **How would you complete this sentence? Say it aloud to a partner.**

   In the morning, I determine what the weather will be by _____.

2. **Which of these sentences describes a person who did <u>not</u> *determine* something? Circle your answer.**

   a. Sam looked in a plant book to find the name of the flower growing in his yard.
   b. From the tracks in the mud, Alysia knew that a raccoon had eaten the cat food.
   c. A look in the microscope told Esteban that the water contained tiny animals.
   d. Tasha took her puppy to obedience training.

3. **Think of a tool or an instrument. Tell what it can help you *determine*.**

   _____

   _____

Name _____

Day 3 determine

1. How would you complete this sentence? Say it aloud to a partner.

The amount of money I save will determine _____.

2. Which of these is <u>not</u> a meaning of *determine*? Circle your answer.

a. to focus

b. to cause

c. to bring about

d. to have an effect on

3. List three factors that *determine* what you do after school.

a. _____

b. _____

c. _____

Day 4 influence

1. How would you complete these sentences? Say them aloud to a partner.

My friends influence my interests by _____.

The influence of my family on me has been _____.

2. Which sentence does <u>not</u> use *influence* correctly? Circle your answer.

a. They are studying the influence of television viewing on young children.

b. The article about the dangers of lightning has influenced my behavior during storms.

c. Many students are absent today because of influence on their own.

d. The stories my grandpa told about Greece influenced my family's decision to go there.

**3. You should be a positive *influence* in the life of a younger family member.
List three examples of how you might behave.**

a. _____

b. _____

c. _____

Name_____

Day 5 **determine • influence**

Fill in the bubble next to the correct answer.

1. In which sentence could the word *determine* fill in the blank?

Ⓐ I can _____ what the results will be, but I can't be certain.

Ⓑ The results of the exam will _____ our final grade.

Ⓒ Approach every problem with _____.

Ⓓ The noises from outside are a _____ to my studying.

2. Which sentence uses *determined* correctly?

Ⓕ I tried to determined the number of fish in the tank.

Ⓖ Put a cup of determined in the washer.

Ⓗ Because I determined the solution, I can't solve the problem.

Ⓙ We determined who left the package on our porch.

3. In which sentence could *influence* replace the underlined words?

Ⓐ I want to <u>have an effect on</u> your decision.

Ⓑ We should try to <u>gain an understanding of</u> other cultures.

Ⓒ Kristen would like to <u>participate in</u> field hockey this year.

Ⓓ Our class likes to <u>talk about</u> the books we read.

Parrots always have a positive **influence** on people.

4. Which sentence does <u>not</u> use *influence* correctly?

Ⓕ The amount of sleep I get has an influence on my mood.

Ⓖ The stream has an influence of pollution from the power plant.

Ⓗ The influence of parents on their children cannot be overestimated.

Ⓙ Historians argue about the influence of weather on the outcome of the battle.

Writing What factors do you think will *determine* what you will choose as a job in your adult years? Be sure to use at least one of this week's words in your writing.

_____

_____

_____

_____

respond • response
elaborate

Use the reproducible definitions on page 190 and the suggestions on page 6 to introduce the words for each day.

DAY 1

respond
(verb) To reply or give an answer. *The students respond in unison to the teacher's questions.*

Test students' familiarity with this word by asking: *When you are introduced to someone you've never met before, how do you respond?* Students may suggest, "It's nice to meet you." Say: *We respond to requests, we respond to questions, we respond to situations, and we respond to invitations.* Ask random questions, and ask students to respond. Then have students complete the Day 1 activities on page 143. You may want to do the first one as a group.

DAY 2

response
(noun) A written or spoken answer or reply. *Peter's response to Mr. Kowal's question was polite and to the point.*

Say: *When we respond, we give a response. When we receive an e-mail from a friend and send an e-mail back, we have sent a response. Our answer to a question, or a reply to any remark, is a response.* Ask: *How else can you give a response?* (e.g., nonverbal nod; gesture) Then say: *Your answers were your responses to my question.* Have students complete the Day 2 activities on page 143. You may want to do the first one as a group.

DAY 3

elaborate
(verb) To add details to something or explain more fully. *Your story would be more interesting if you would elaborate on the character description.*

Pronounce the word, being especially careful to clearly say the long "a" in the final syllable. Say: *When someone asks, "Could you elaborate on that?" they want to hear more.* Then say: *Pretend I ask you what kind of school you go to. You say, "I go to a good school." How would you reply if I asked you to elaborate on your response?* Then have students complete the Day 3 activities on page 144. You may want to do the first one as a group.

DAY 4

elaborate
(adj.) Complicated; detailed. *The design for the treehouse is elaborate because it includes shutters and window boxes.*

Point out the difference in pronunciation from Day 3. Draw a simple design on the board, and then draw an elaborate design, one with many twists, turns, and curls. Ask: *Which design is elaborate? Why is it elaborate?* Then say: *Plans can also be elaborate.* Ask: *How could your plans for a party be elaborate? Describe those elaborate plans.* Then have students complete the Day 4 activities on page 144. You may want to do the first one as a group.

DAY 5

Have students complete page 145. Call on students to read aloud their answers to the writing activity.

Day 1 respond

1. How would you complete this sentence? Say it aloud to a partner.

I respond to my teacher's questions by _____.

2. Which of the following words are synonyms for *respond*? Circle your answers.

a. answer   c. complain

b. question   d. reply

3. Which sentence does <u>not</u> use *respond* correctly? Circle your answer.

a. Please respond to the questions on this exam by writing complete sentences.

b. The mayor responded to my letter by calling me on the phone.

c. The respond was not the answer I expected.

d. Our principal will always respond to a polite question.

4. How would you *respond* if asked to describe your favorite animal?

_____

_____

Day 2 response

1. How would you complete this sentence? Say it aloud to a partner.

To give a "yes" response, I could _____.

**2. The question on the test is "What is the northernmost place on our planet?"
Circle the correct *response.***

a. North America   c. Africa

b. North Pole   d. Australia

3. In which sentences could *response* fill in the blank? Circle your answers.

a. He will _____ to my greeting with a nod and a wave of his hand.

b. The senator gave a brief _____ to the reporter's question.

c. She relaxed on the sofa in an attitude of _____.

d. In _____ to my request for an interview, the actor shook his head.

Day 3 elaborate

1. How would you complete this sentence? Say it aloud to a partner.

I can elaborate on how to _____.

2. Which sentence describes someone who is *elaborating* on a subject? Circle your answer.

    a. Miss Bruno described in detail how she wrote the new song for the choir.

    b. The nervous student replied briefly to her teacher's questions about the science project.

    c. Lynette spelled her last name, gave her address, and said no more.

    d. Jerome replied to his friend's question by saying that the subject did not interest him.

3. Which sentence uses *elaborate* correctly? Circle your answer.

    a. In the elaborate, the chemists carefully measure their chemicals.

    b. The treasurer elaborated on the budget by listing the club's debts.

    c. The student elaborated by saying, "I don't know."

    d. The runoff from the power plant is sure to elaborate the river.

Day 4 elaborate

1. How would you complete this sentence? Say it aloud to a partner.

The most elaborate costume I've ever seen was _____.

2. Which word is an antonym of *elaborate?* Circle your answer.

    a. wonderful   c. complicated

    b. failed   d. simple

3. Which sentence does <u>not</u> use *elaborate* correctly? Circle your answer.

    a. The elaborate design for the bridge included special bolts and steel supports.

    b. The elaborate table setting included special forks for the salad and for the dessert.

    c. Because he had run the marathon, he was elaborated.

    d. The set for the school play was elaborate and included a bridge and a waterfall.

4. Describe the most *elaborate* school project you've ever worked on.

_____

_____

_____

Name_____

Day 5 respond • response • elaborate

Fill in the bubble next to the correct answer.

1. In which sentence could *respond* replace the underlined word or words?

Ⓐ The judges <u>reject</u> entries to the contest that do not meet the basic requirements.

Ⓑ Liz could not <u>think about</u> the problem without being upset.

Ⓒ It was the <u>quick thinking</u> of the conductor that saved the train from the collision.

Ⓓ I will <u>give an answer</u> after I have carefully thought about the question.

2. Your *response* to a party invitation is expected. What should you do?

Ⓕ invite your cousin to come with you

Ⓖ call the host to tell him that you will be there

Ⓗ shop for new jeans, a shirt, and shoes to wear

Ⓙ bring a cake and a present to the party

3. Which sentence uses *elaborate* correctly?

Ⓐ The detective in the story elaborated on his reasons for suspecting the butler.

Ⓑ The mouse made its way through the elaborate and came out the other side.

Ⓒ Since the coach asked me to elaborate, I gave her the shortest answer that I could.

Ⓓ The elaborate of this homework assignment has confused me.

4. Which of these activities would most likely <u>not</u> require *elaborate* preparation?

Ⓕ building a skyscraper

Ⓖ walking to the store to buy milk

Ⓗ preparing a science project that includes an experiment

Ⓙ planning a carnival with games, rides, and food

Writing   How would you *respond* to someone's invitation to sail around the world? *Elaborate* on your *response*. Be sure to use at least one of this week's words in your writing.

_____

_____

_____

_____

category • categorize
consist • constitute

Use the reproducible definitions on page 191 and the suggestions on page 6 to introduce the words for each day.

DAY 1

category
(noun) A class or group of things that have something in common. *I place books about history in one category and biographies in another.*

Say: *When I sort a pile of papers and put all the spelling tests in one pile and all the math homework into another pile, I put the papers into categories.* Ask: *What are some categories, or classes, of animals?* (e.g., mammals; reptiles) Then ask: *Why do we put things into categories?* (e.g., to be able to look at like things; to organize) Then have students complete the Day 1 activities on page 147. You may want to do the first one as a group.

DAY 2

categorize
(verb) To place or arrange things into categories. *I categorize my photos by event.*

Say: *When we put things or people into categories, we categorize them.* Write these words on the board: "fable, solve, problem, vowels, subtract, pronounce." Ask: *What are some ways we can categorize these words?* (e.g., by part of speech; by subject) Encourage students to use the word **categorize** in their suggestions. Have volunteers write the categories and the words in them on the board. Then have students complete the Day 2 activities on page 147. You may want to do the first one as a group.

DAY 3

consist
(verb) To be made up or formed. *The art show consists of works created by middle school students.*

Tell students that when we think about what something **consists** of, we are thinking about the parts that make up a whole. Say: *A year consists of twelve months.* Ask: *Are there other ways to break a year into parts?* Encourage students to use the sentence starter, "A year **consists** of ___." Students may reply that a year **consists** of four seasons, or 52 weeks, or 365 days. Then have students complete the Day 3 activities on page 148. You may want to do the first one as a group.

DAY 4

constitute
(verb) To form or make up. *Grades nine through twelve constitute the high school.*

Say: *You know that a year consists of twelve months. We could also say that twelve months constitute a year.* Tell students that **constitute** is another way of saying "made up of." Ask: *What would you say constitutes a classroom? What must a room have in order to be a classroom?* (e.g., a teacher and students) Then have students complete the Day 4 activities on page 148. You may want to do the first one as a group.

DAY 5

Have students complete page 149. Call on students to read aloud their answers to the writing activity.

Name_____

Day 1 category

1. **How would you complete this sentence? Say it aloud to a partner.**

   I can answer trivia questions in the _____ category.

2. **Which sentences use *category* correctly? Circle your answers.**

   a. The musician is playing that song on a category.
   b. I'm organizing my DVDs by sorting them into categories.
   c. Into which category would you put *Treasure Island?*
   d. I watch as the twins category their toys into piles.

3. **In which sentence could *category* replace the underlined word? Circle your answer.**

   a. Jared and Sam think that this movie is too scary to watch again.
   b. If you sort the notebooks into piles, I will put them away.
   c. I will decide in which type of music this song belongs.
   d. The secretary files the records in alphabetical order.

Day 2 categorize

1. **How would you complete this sentence? Say it aloud to a partner.**

   I can categorize a shopping list by _____.

2. **Which one is not a way to *categorize* trees? Circle your answer.**

   a. height   c. speed
   b. width   d. age

3. **In which places are you not likely to find things *categorized*? Circle your answers.**

   a. mountain   c. beach
   b. library   d. drugstore

4. **What are some ways you can *categorize* historical events?**

   _____

   _____

   _____

Name _____

Day 3 | consist

1. How would you complete this sentence? Say it aloud to a partner.

My favorite meal consists of _____.

2. Which sentence uses *consist* correctly? Circle your answer.

   a. A peninsula is a landmass that consists into water.
   b. Patty consists that we play the game her way.
   c. You must consist your work if you want to succeed.
   d. This orchard consists of apple trees and pear trees.

3. In which sentence could *consist* fill in the blank? Circle your answer.

   a. Lively cities _____ of homes, businesses, parks, and people.
   b. It is kind to _____ those in need.
   c. In a _____, the school bell will ring, and it will be time to begin work.
   d. When someone tells you to do something that is wrong, you must _____.

4. What does your typical school day *consist* of?

_____

_____

Day 4 | constitute

1. How would you complete this sentence? Say it aloud to a partner.

_____, _____, and _____ constitute a great vacation.

2. Which word or phrase could fill in the blank in this sentence? Circle your answer.

Reading, math, science, geography, and history constitute _____.

   a. all over the country   c. a day at school
   b. problems   d. in six hours

3. List three activities that together *constitute* your homework routine.

   a. _____

   b. _____

   c. _____

Name_____

Day 5 category • categorize • consist • constitute

Fill in the bubble next to the correct answer.

1. Which word is a synonym for *category*?

- Ⓐ variation
- Ⓑ elementary
- Ⓒ mistake
- Ⓓ class

2. Which phrase describes what you are doing when you are *categorizing*?

- Ⓕ moving things
- Ⓖ arranging things into groups
- Ⓗ taking someone else's ideas
- Ⓙ running into trouble

3. Which sentence does <u>not</u> use *consist* correctly?

- Ⓐ Ice cream consists of cream, sugar, and flavoring.
- Ⓑ My day consisted of going to school, playing hockey, and doing homework.
- Ⓒ The exam will consist of three parts.
- Ⓓ The amusement park consists that young children not be allowed on certain rides.

4. Which sentence uses *constitute* correctly?

- Ⓕ My shelf constitutes books and binders.
- Ⓖ These players constitute a winning team.
- Ⓗ Car horns constitute in a busy city.
- Ⓙ Warm cookies and cold milk are a good constitute.

Writing   Into what *categories* would you place the things in your room at home? Do you have special places for different *categories* of things? Use at least one of this week's words in your writing.

_____

_____

_____

_____

CUMULATIVE REVIEW
WORDS FROM WEEKS 28–35

associate
association
categorize
category
conform
consist
consistency
consistent
constant
constitute
correspond
correspondence
corresponding
determine
differentiate
discriminate
distinct
distinction
elaborate
influence
relationship
relative to
represent
representative
respond
response
symbol
symbolic
symbolize

Days 1–4

Each day's activity is a cloze paragraph that students complete with words or forms of words that they have learned in weeks 28–35. Before students begin, pronounce each word in the box on the student page, have students repeat each word, and then review each word's meaning(s). **Other ways to review the words:**

- Start a sentence containing one of the words and have students finish the sentence orally. For example:

    I **associate** Saturdays with…
    I **respond** to a compliment by…

- Provide students with a definition and ask them to supply the word that fits it.

- Ask questions that require students to know the meaning of each word. For example:

    What factors **determine** how you dress for the day?
    In your opinion, what **constitutes** a great meal?

- Have students use each word in a sentence.

Day 5

Start by reviewing the words in the crossword puzzle activity for Day 5. Write the words on the board and have students repeat them after you. Provide a sentence for one of the words. Ask students to think of their own sentence and share it with a partner. Call on several students to share their sentences. Follow the same procedure for the remaining words. Then have students complete the crossword activity.

Extension Ideas

Use any of the following activities to help integrate the vocabulary words into other content areas:

- Have students **determine** how they can **discriminate** between an Asian elephant and an African elephant.

- Have students create a coat of arms for their family, choosing **symbols** that **symbolize** the traits and characteristics of their families.

- Have students **correspond** with students in another country. Encourage them to **elaborate** on their daily lives and what they learn in school.

- Have students examine **relationships** between cultures and native dances or music.

Daily Academic Vocabulary

categorized	constituted	determines	influenced	symbolized
consistent	corresponded	elaborate	represented	symbols

Day 1

Fill in the blanks with words from the word box.

If you had to choose an object to stand for your family, what would it be? As

early as the 1100s, knights chose coats of arms that _____

their families. A coat of arms is made up of many images, colors, and

_____. Sometimes words _____ a coat of

arms, too. These works of art _____, or matched, with the

characteristics and honors of a family. For example, a lion on a coat of arms

_____ the courage of a family. The knights wore the coats of

arms on their shields when they went into battle or competed in tournaments.

Day 2

Fill in the blanks with words from the word box.

Books in many libraries are _____ by the Dewey Decimal

System. A book's place is decided by its topic. This _____ where

it will be placed in the library. Melvil Dewey was a librarian who created the system

in the 1870s. At the time, libraries used different methods to organize books.

This lack of a _____ organization of books affected Dewey. It

_____ his development of this detailed and _____

system into which books are placed. The Dewey Decimal System is now used in

95 percent of all school and public libraries.

| associated | category | consist | correspondence | relative to |
| association | conform | consistency | distinct | |

Day 3

Fill in the blanks with words from the word box.

Last year, my class exchanged letters with a class at a school in Ecuador. The

_____ taught us about the importance of bananas in that South

American country. Most families _____ of at least one banana

farmer. I never connected the yellow fruit to farming before. I _____

them with the grocery store. We learned how bananas are different from other

foods. Besides having a _____ taste, they grow on tall plants that

can have 30-foot-long leaves. _____ other fruits, bananas are

extremely popular. The average person eats 33 pounds of bananas a year!

Day 4

Fill in the blanks with words from the word box.

Isabella's favorite _____ of sports includes those played

in water. However, she considers surfing the most exciting. She connects

it to excitement and summertime. This _____ comes from

summers spent in the ocean with her father. She also feels surfing is challenging

because waves never _____ to a pattern. This lack of

_____ makes it more difficult than sports like skateboarding, in

which the surface doesn't move. Even though surfing is hard sometimes, she can't

imagine life without her surfboard.

Name_____

Daily Academic Vocabulary

Crossword Challenge

For each clue, write one of the words from the word box to complete the puzzle.

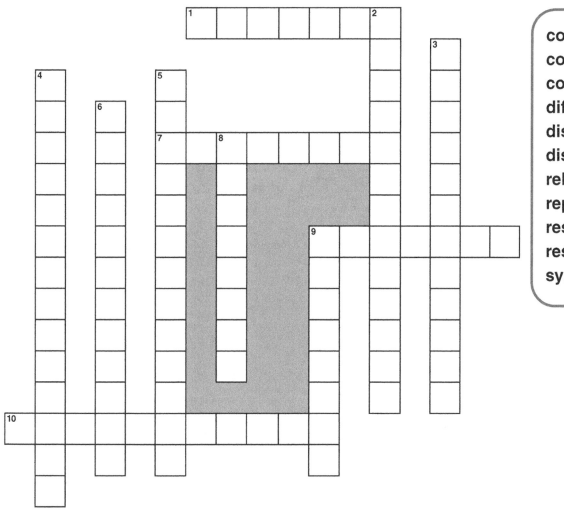

Word Box

conform
constant
corresponding
differentiate
discriminate
distinction
relationship
representative
respond
response
symbolic

Across

1. to reply
7. a written or spoken answer
9. to act in a way that agrees with a rule or standard
10. a feature that makes something different from another

Down

2. to find or see differences or distinctions
3. the way in which things are connected
4. a person or thing that is typical of a group
5. in agreement or matching with
6. to see a clear difference
8. acting as a symbol
9. going on without stopping

Answer Key

Week 1

Day 1
2. Answers will vary.
3. a, c

Day 2
2. d
3. Answers will vary.
4. Answers will vary.

Day 3
2. a
3. a, c
4. Answers will vary.

Day 4
2. b, c
3. Answers will vary.

Day 5
1. B   2. H   3. C   4. G

Week 2

Day 1
2. b
3. d
4. Answers will vary.

Day 2
2. c
3. d, b, a, c

Day 3
2. d
3. b
4. Answers will vary.

Day 4
2. c
3. a

Day 5
1. C   2. J   3. C   4. H

Week 3

Day 1
2. c
3. b, d

Day 2
2. a
3. Answers will vary.
4. Answers will vary.

Day 3
2. a, c
3. c
4. Answers will vary.

Day 4
2. d
3. Answers will vary.

Day 5
1. D   2. G   3. C   4. F

Week 4

Day 1
2. c
3. d
4. Answers will vary.

Day 2
2. d
3. b

Day 3
2. Answers will vary.
3. d
4. Answers will vary.

Day 4
2. b, c
3. c

Day 5
1. B   2. H   3. C   4. J

Week 5

Day 1
2. c
3. d
4. Answers will vary.

Day 2
2. Answers will vary.
3. d

Day 3
2. b
3. c

Day 4
2. Answers will vary.
3. a
4. Answers will vary.

Day 5
1. B   2. F   3. B   4. H

Week 6

Day 1
2. c
3. a
4. Answers will vary.

Day 2
2. b
3. a

Day 3
2. c
3. b
4. Answers will vary.

Day 4
2. c
3. a, b

Day 5
1. B   2. J   3. C   4. J

Week 7

Day 1
2. b
3. b

Day 2
2. b, a, d, c
3. d

Day 3
2. c
3. a
4. Answers will vary.

Day 4
2. b, d
3. c, d

Day 5
1. C   2. G   3. C   4. H

Week 8

Day 1
2. c
3. d

Day 2
2. a
3. Answers will vary.
4. Answers will vary.

Day 3
2. d
3. a, b

Day 4
2. b, d
3. b, c
Day 5
1. B   2. F   3. C   4. J

Review Week 9

Day 1
typical, translated, interpreted, perform, accomplishment
Day 2
presumed, contended, persuaded, translation, interpretation
Day 3
quotation, estimation, standard, calculate, assume
Day 4
implied, performances, convinced, persuasive, accomplished
Day 5
1. quote
2. estimate
3. implication
4. assumption
5. persuasion
6. suppose
7. clarify
code: the emperor penguin

Week 10

Day 1
2. a
3. b
Day 2
2. Answers will vary.
3. d
Day 3
2. c
3. a
Day 4
2. Answers will vary.
3. b
Day 5
1. A   2. H   3. C   4. F

Week 11

Day 1
2. a, d
3. Answers will vary.
4. c
Day 2
2. Answers will vary.
3. c
Day 3
2. b, d
3. c
4. Answers will vary.
Day 4
2. b
3. b
Day 5
1. A   2. H   3. D   4. G

Week 12

Day 1
2. a
3. d
4. Answers will vary.
Day 2
2. d
3. a
Day 3
2. b
3. a
Day 4
2. b
3. c
4. Answers will vary.
Day 5
1. D   2. G   3. A   4. H

Week 13

Day 1
2. c
3. Answers will vary.
4. Answers will vary.
Day 2
2. c
3. b
Day 3
2. b
3. a
4. Answers will vary.

Day 4
2. b
3. c
Day 5
1. D   2. G   3. B   4. G

Week 14

Day 1
2. c
3. Answers will vary.
4. Answers will vary.
Day 2
2. b
3. b, d
Day 3
2. a, d
3. c
4. Answers will vary.
Day 4
2. b, c
3. d
Day 5
1. B   2. H   3. B   4. J

Week 15

Day 1
2. d
3. Answers will vary.
Day 2
2. a, b
3. a, d
4. Answers will vary.
Day 3
2. a, d
3. Answers will vary.
4. Answers will vary.
Day 4
2. b, d
3. d
Day 5
1. D   2. J   3. C   4. H

Week 16

Day 1
2. d
3. c

Day 2
2. Answers will vary.
3. b, c
4. Answers will vary.
Day 3
2. Answers will vary.
3. d
Day 4
2. b
3. c
Day 5
1. A   2. G   3. A   4. H

Week 17

Day 1
2. c
3. d
4. Answers will vary.
Day 2
2. c
3. a
Day 3
2. d
3. Answers will vary.
Day 4
2. a
3. c
Day 5
1. B   2. H   3. D   4. G

Review Week 18

Day 1
position, development,
in detail, applicable,
information
Day 2
informed, specific,
applications, details,
evidence
Day 3
specify, complicated or
complex, designate, defends
Day 4
perspective, applied,
develop, complex or
complicated

Day 5
Down
1. reference
3. evident
4. viewpoint
6. assign
7. complicate
Across
2. delegate
5. refer
8. complication
9. assignment

Week 19

Day 1
2. c
3. b
4. Answers will vary.
Day 2
2. a, d
3. b
Day 3
2. c
3. a
Day 4
2. a, d
3. Answers will vary.
Day 5
1. B   2. H   3. D   4. F

Week 20

Day 1
2. c
3. a, d
Day 2
2. a, c
3. d
Day 3
2. a, c
3. Answers will vary.
Day 4
2. b
3. b, d
4. Answers will vary.
Day 5
1. C   2. J   3. A   4. G

Week 21

Day 1
2. b
3. a, d
Day 2
2. d
3. c
4. Answers will vary.
Day 3
2. a, d
3. b
Day 4
2. d
3. Answers will vary.
Day 5
1. B   2. F   3. C   4. G

Week 22

Day 1
2. c
3. b
4. Answers will vary.
Day 2
2. c
3. a
Day 3
2. a
3. b
4. Answers will vary.
Day 4
2. d
3. b, d
Day 5
1. D   2. G   3. B   4. F

Week 23

Day 1
2. b
3. a, c
Day 2
2. c
3. d
4. Answers will vary.
Day 3
2. d
3. Answers will vary.
Day 4
2. b, d
3. b

Day 5
1. C   2. J   3. B   4. F

Week 24

Day 1
2. a
3. c
4. Answers will vary.

Day 2
2. b, c
3. Answers will vary.

Day 3
2. Answers will vary.
3. a

Day 4
2. d
3. Answers will vary.

Day 5
1. D   2. F   3. C   4. H

Week 25

Day 1
2. a, c
3. c
4. Answers will vary.

Day 2
2. b, c
3. a, c

Day 3
2. c
3. a, d
4. Answers will vary.

Day 4
2. a, d
3. a

Day 5
1. D   2. G   3. D   4. H

Week 26

Day 1
2. c
3. a, b

Day 2
2. b
3. Answers will vary.
4. Answers will vary.

Day 3
2. c
3. d

Day 4
2. b
3. a, c
4. Answers will vary.

Day 5
1. C   2. F   3. C   4. G

Review Week 27

Day 1
prevalent, significance, accuracy, critical, imitation

Day 2
insignificant, address, substitute, dominant, primary

Day 3
topic, significant, aspects, emphasis, precision

Day 4
emphasize, factor, accurate, modified

Day 5
1. condition
2. imitate
3. criticism
4. focus
5. critique
6. pattern
7. precise
8. prevalent
code: herpetologist

Week 28

Day 1
2. c
3. a, c
4. Answers will vary.

Day 2
2. b
3. d

Day 3
2. b, d
3. a, d
4. Answers will vary.

Day 4
2. b, c
3. a

Day 5
1. D   2. F   3. B   4. J

Week 29

Day 1
2. a, d
3. d
4. Answers will vary.

Day 2
2. a
3. d

Day 3
2. d
3. b, c

Day 4
2. b
3. c
4. Answers will vary.

Day 5
1. C   2. G   3. A   4. J

Week 30

Day 1
2. c
3. a, d

Day 2
2. c
3. b, d
4. circle, square, rectangle, oval

Day 3
2. a
3. c

Day 4
2. Answers will vary.
3. d

Day 5
1. D   2. H   3. B   4. H

Week 31

Day 1
2. a
3. b
4. Answers will vary.

Day 2
2. c
3. d

Day 3
2. a, c
3. Answers will vary.

Day 4
2. a
3. Answers will vary.
4. Answers will vary.

Day 5
1. B   2. H   3. D   4. H

Week 32

Day 1
2. b
3. d
4. addition, multiplication, division, equals

Day 2
2. b
3. a

Day 3
2. d
3. a, c

Day 4
2. b, d, a, c
3. Answers will vary.

Day 5
1. C   2. J   3. A   4. H

Week 33

Day 1
2. a, c
3. d

Day 2
2. d
3. Answers will vary.

Day 3
2. a
3. Answers will vary.

Day 4
2. c
3. Answers will vary.

Day 5
1. B   2. J   3. A   4. G

Week 34

Day 1
2. a, d
3. c
4. Answers will vary.

Day 2
2. b
3. b, d

Day 3
2. a
3. b

Day 4
2. d
3. c
4. Answers will vary.

Day 5
1. D   2. G   3. A   4. G

Week 35

Day 1
2. b, c
3. c

Day 2
2. c
3. a, c
4. Answers will vary.

Day 3
2. d
3. a
4. Answers will vary.

Day 4
2. c
3. Answers will vary.

Day 5
1. D   2. G   3. D   4. G

Review Week 36

Day 1
represented, symbols, constituted, corresponded, symbolized

Day 2
categorized, determines, consistent, influenced, elaborate

Day 3
correspondence, consist, associated, distinct, Relative to

Day 4
category, association, conform, consistency

Day 5
  Across
    1. respond
    7. response
    9. conform
    10. distinction

Down
  2. differentiate
  3. relationship
  4. representative
  5. corresponding
  6. discriminate
  8. symbolic
  9. constant

Index

accomplish   26, 42
accomplishment   26, 42
accuracy   98, 114
accurate   98, 114
address   110, 114
applicable   66, 78
application   66, 78
apply   66, 78
aspect   86, 114
assign   62, 78
assignment   62, 78
associate   118, 150
association   118, 150
assume   14, 42
assumption   14, 42
calculate   38, 42
categorize   146, 150
category   146, 150
clarify   34, 42
complex   54, 78
complicate   54, 78
complicated   54, 78
complication   54, 78
condition   86, 114
conform   126, 150
consist   146, 150
consistency   122, 150
consistent   122, 150
constant   122, 150
constitute   146, 150
contend   22, 42
convince   18, 42
correspond   126, 150
correspondence   126, 150
corresponding   126, 150
critical   106, 114
criticism   106, 114

critique   106, 114
defend   58, 78
delegate   62, 78
designate   62, 78
detail   50, 78
determine   138, 150
develop   74, 78
development   74, 78
differentiate   130, 150
discriminate   130, 150
distinct   130, 150
distinction   130, 150
dominant   102, 114
elaborate   142, 150
emphasis   82, 114
emphasize   82, 114
estimate   38, 42
estimation   38, 42
evidence   70, 78
evident   70, 78
factor   86, 114
focus   110, 114
imitate   94, 114
imitation   94, 114
implication   22, 42
imply   22, 42
in detail   50, 78
influence   138, 150
inform   70, 78
information   70, 78
insignificant   82, 114
interpret   34, 42
interpretation   34, 42
modification   90, 114
modify   90, 114
pattern   94, 114
perform   26, 42

performance   26, 42
perspective   58, 78
persuade   18, 42
persuasion   18, 42
persuasive   18, 42
position   58, 78
precise   98, 114
precision   98, 114
presume   14, 42
prevalent   102, 114
primary   102, 114
quotation   30, 42
quote   30, 42
refer   46, 78
reference   46, 78
relationship   118, 150
relative to   118, 150
represent   134, 150
representative   134, 150
respond   142, 150
response   142, 150
significance   82, 114
significant   82, 114
specific   50, 78
specify   50, 78
standard   10, 42
substitute   90, 114
suppose   14, 42
symbol   134, 150
symbolic   134, 150
symbolize   134, 150
topic   110, 114
translate   30, 42
translation   30, 42
typical   10, 42
viewpoint   58, 78

typical

(adj.) Showing the traits or characteristics that are normal for a certain thing.

*Yesterday was a **typical** school day.*

standard

(adj.) Normal or regular; typical.

*"Hello" is the **standard** greeting on the telephone.*

standard

(noun) A model or example used to determine how good other things are.

*Our best player's kicking sets a high **standard** for the rest of the team.*

standard

(adj.) Widely accepted as a rule or model.

*The **standard** procedure for a fire drill requires us to move quickly and quietly.*

Daily Academic Vocabulary • EMC 2761 • © Evan-Moor Corporation

suppose   DAY 1

(verb)	To believe; to think.	*I **suppose** that I could do better on tests if I studied more.*

assume   DAY 2

(verb)	To take a duty, job, or responsibility upon yourself.	*As an older brother, I always **assume** the responsibility of watching out for my younger sister.*

assume • assumption   DAY 3

assume

(verb)	To suppose that something is right without checking it.	*I **assume** we will practice on Sunday.*

assumption

(noun)	Something that is supposed, expected, or taken for granted.	*My **assumption** is that the story will have a happy ending.*

presume   DAY 4

(verb)	To think that something is true without really knowing or having all the facts.	*A jury must **presume** that defendants are innocent until evidence proves them guilty.*

convince

(verb) To make someone believe or accept something.

*Raul **convinced** me to choose him as president of our gamers club.*

persuade

(verb) To convince someone to do or believe something.

*Please **persuade** your sister to wear a raincoat today.*

persuasion

(noun) The act of convincing; the ability to convince someone to do or believe something.

*A good salesperson has strong skills of **persuasion**.*

persuasive

(adj.) Having the ability to cause someone to do or believe something.

*Her **persuasive** speech convinced us to vote for her.*

imply

(verb) To suggest or mean something without actually saying it.

*When you use an angry tone of voice, you **imply** that you are upset.*

implication

(noun) Something suggested, but not actually said.

*The **implication** of the frown on his face was that his answer was "no."*

implication

(noun) The meaning or importance of something; consequences.

*The **implications** of the new highway were alarming to the people living near it.*

contend

(verb) To argue or claim.

*My sister **contends** that she never borrowed my bike.*

perform

(verb) To carry out or do something.

*Planning the day's activities is one task that schoolteachers **perform**.*

performance

(noun) The way in which a job or action is carried out.

*A test can be used to measure the **performance** of the students in the class.*

accomplish

(verb) To carry out or do something successfully.

*I hope to **accomplish** many things today.*

accomplishment

(noun) Something that has been done successfully.

*Your perfect score on the test was a great **accomplishment**.*

translate

(verb) To say in another language or change into other words.

*I will **translate** my friend's words from Spanish into English for him.*

translation

(noun) A changing of something from one language to another.

*Our class read an English **translation** of the original French story.*

quote

(verb) To repeat words that were spoken or written by someone else.

*Mr. Sanchez will often **quote** passages from his favorite poems.*

quotation

(noun) Words that are repeated exactly as spoken or written by someone else.

*A **quotation** from the mayor appeared on the front page of the paper.*

interpret　　　　　　　　　　　　　　　　　　　　　　　　DAY 1

(verb)　To explain the meaning of something.　　　*Our teacher helped us **interpret** the poem.*

interpretation　　　　　　　　　　　　　　　　　　　　DAY 2

(noun)　An explanation of the meaning of something.　　*Dr. Zee's **interpretation** of the test results surprised the other doctors.*

interpret　　　　　　　　　　　　　　　　　　　　　　　　DAY 3

(verb)　To orally translate from one language to another.　*Yuri will **interpret** for his Russian-speaking father.*

clarify　　　　　　　　　　　　　　　　　　　　　　　　DAY 4

(verb)　To make something clear.　　*The diagram will **clarify** how to assemble the bookshelf.*

estimate

(verb) To make a careful guess about something.

*I **estimate** that it will take an hour to complete my work.*

estimate

(noun) A careful guess about the amount, size, cost, or value of something.

*My **estimate** is that we will need three students for this project.*

estimation

(noun) An opinion; judgment.

*In my **estimation**, nothing is better to eat than ice cream.*

calculate

(verb) To find out an answer or result by using mathematics.

*I can **calculate** the total cost of the trip based on the number of students who will be going.*

refer

(verb) To speak of, mention, or call attention to someone or something.

*Books often **refer** to famous events in history.*

reference

(noun) A mention of someone or something.

*There was a **reference** to our school in the newspaper yesterday.*

refer

(verb) To turn to for help or information.

***Refer** to the encyclopedia for facts about the country of Brazil.*

reference

(noun) A source of information.

*My grammar handbook is a good **reference** for the rules of punctuation.*

specify • specific

specify

(verb)	To name or say something exactly.	*Mr. Winter will **specify** which problems we have to do for homework.*

specific

(adj.)	Particular, definite, or individually named.	*Please show me the **specific** book that you want to read.*

detail

(noun)	A small part of a whole thing.	*I missed that **detail** about the party because I read the invitation too quickly.*

detail

(verb)	To describe or tell very precisely.	*I will **detail** each step in the process so that you will know exactly what to do.*

in detail

(adv. phrase)	Thoroughly, with attention to specifics.	*William described **in detail** everything he had done on his vacation.*

complicate • complicated

complicate

(verb)	To make something more difficult to do or understand.	*If you forget to bring your lunch, it will **complicate** our day.*

complicated

(adj.)	Hard to understand or difficult to do.	*All of the questions on the test are too **complicated** to answer.*

complication

(noun)	A difficulty that causes a problem.	*When her car broke down, finding another way to get to work was a **complication** for my mother.*

complex

(adj.)	Made up of many parts.	*Automobiles are **complex** machines.*

complex

(adj.)	Very difficult to understand or do.	*This game is too **complex** for younger kids.*

defend

(verb) To argue or speak in support of something.

*The school board members **defend** their decision to make the school day longer.*

viewpoint

(noun) An opinion or way of thinking about something.

*My friend and I share a common **viewpoint** on many subjects.*

position

(noun) A person's opinion or point of view on an issue or subject.

*I took the **position** that we should recycle paper in our classroom.*

perspective

(noun) A particular view or way of looking at something.

*From my mom's **perspective**, my music is too loud.*

assign • assignment

assign

(verb) To give as a task or duty.

*Why do teachers **assign** homework that is due on Monday?*

---

assignment

(noun) A specific job or task that is given to somebody.

*My dad's **assignment** was to clean out the garage.*

assign

(verb) To set apart or give out for a particular use.

*The librarians **assign** these shelves for the books on music.*

delegate

(verb) To give someone else the responsibility to do something.

*Our parents **delegate** the small chores to my sister and me.*

designate

(verb) To choose for a particular job or purpose.

*Our teacher will **designate** someone to erase the board.*

apply

(verb)   To put into action
or use.

*In this experiment, you will **apply** what you learned
yesterday about liquids.*

application

(noun)   A way of being
used.

*Electricity has many **applications** in our lives.*

apply

(verb)   To be suitable for;
to have to do with
something.

*The rules of conduct **apply** to everyone in the
classroom.*

applicable

(adj.)   Being well suited
for something.

*Your advice is **applicable** to many situations.*

inform

(verb) To tell or give information to someone.

*I will **inform** the school that you are ill.*

information

(noun) Knowledge or facts about something.

*Martin gathered **information** for his report on the planet Saturn.*

evidence

(noun) Information or facts that help prove something or make you believe that it is true.

*Scientists are still looking for **evidence** of life on other planets.*

evident

(adj.) Easy to see and understand; obvious.

*It is **evident** from your test scores that you have been studying harder.*

develop

(verb) To make something more complex or effective.

*The students will **develop** the homework assignment into a project for the science fair.*

develop

(verb) To grow or become stronger.

*Small sand piles often **develop** into large sand dunes as a result of high winds.*

development

(noun) The act or process of bringing something to a completed state.

*I think your story needs further **development** before you turn it in.*

development

(noun) An important event or happening.

*The newscaster announced the latest **development** in the story.*

significance

(noun) The importance or meaning of something.

*Everyone at the picnic table understood the **significance** of the darkening clouds.*

significant • insignificant

significant

(adj.) Important, or having great meaning.

*The captain made the most **significant** contribution to the team.*

insignificant

(adj.) Not important, or having very little meaning.

*The color of the bicycle is **insignificant** to the racer.*

emphasis

(noun) Special attention or importance given to something.

*The history book's **emphasis** was on the causes of the war, not the results.*

emphasize

(verb) To give emphasis or importance to something.

*My parents **emphasize** the importance of good manners.*

condition

(noun) The general state of being of someone or something.

*You must return borrowed books in good **condition**.*

condition

(noun) Something that is needed before another thing can happen.

*You may attend the carnival on the **condition** that you clean your room.*

factor

(noun) Something that influences a result.

*The weather was a **factor** in the outcome of the sailboat race.*

aspect

(noun) One particular feature or characteristic of something.

*Consider every **aspect** of the problem before suggesting a solution.*

modify

(verb) To change or alter somewhat.

*I will **modify** the dialogue in my story to make it sound more realistic.*

modification

(noun) A change or alteration of something.

*The teacher's **modification** of the assignment made it easier to complete.*

substitute

(verb) To put in the place of another person or thing.

*The coach will **substitute** the rookie for the injured player.*

substitute

(noun) Someone or something that takes the place of another.

*My aunt uses honey in her tea as a **substitute** for sugar.*

pattern

(verb) To make something or to act following a plan or a model.

*The best dancers **pattern** their steps after Ms. Petrie's example.*

imitate

(verb) To copy the actions or appearance of something or someone.

*My little brother **imitates** everything I do.*

imitation

(noun) The act of imitating or copying.

*His **imitation** of a monkey is very funny.*

imitation

(noun) A copy or likeness of something else.

*Kayli saw an **imitation** of the Eiffel Tower in Paris, TN.*

accurate • accuracy

accurate

(adj.) Correct or free from errors.

*Consult the atlas for **accurate** information on the mountain's height.*

accuracy

(noun) The condition of being exact and correct.

*A good newspaper reporter checks the **accuracy** of her information.*

precise

(adj.) Very accurate or exact; definite.

*The schedule tells you the **precise** time that the train will leave the station.*

precise

(adj.) Clearly said or communicated.

*His **precise** response answered the judge's questions.*

precision

(noun) Accuracy or exactness.

*The marching band performed every step of the routine with **precision**.*

primary

(adj.)   Most important;
main or chief.

*The **primary** reason for choosing that jacket was its affordability.*

primary

(adj.)   First in order or time.

*When you start school, you are in the **primary** grades.*

dominant

(adj.)   Most powerful or
important.

*The **dominant** animal in the herd will eat before the others.*

prevalent

(adj.)   Found or happening
frequently;
widespread.

*The cold virus is **prevalent** in the winter months.*

criticism

(noun) The act of judging what is good or bad in something.

*The **criticism** offered by my writing group helped me make my story more interesting.*

critique

(verb) To say what is good or bad about something.

*My older sister often **critiques** my reports.*

critical

(adj.) Very important or serious.

*The right kind of cold weather gear is **critical** for people who live in the arctic regions.*

critical

(adj.) Involving careful evaluation and judgment.

*The boy used **critical** thinking skills to solve the problem.*

address

(verb)   To deal with a problem or situation.

*I will **address** my problem of getting to school on time by getting up earlier.*

address

(verb)   To give a talk or speech.

*The principal will **address** the students at today's assembly.*

focus

(verb)   To put one's attention on something or somebody; concentrate.

*Students should **focus** on their work and try to ignore the noise in the hall.*

focus • topic

focus

(noun)   A center of activity, interest, or attention.

*Ecology will be the **focus** of our science class today.*

topic

(noun)   The subject of a book, essay, or other written work.

*The invention of the light bulb is the **topic** of this report.*

associate

(verb) | To connect with something else in your mind. | *I always **associate** roses with my mother's birthday.*

association

(noun) | The connection of one feeling, thought, or emotion with another. | *I have a strong **association** between lemonade and hot summer days.*

relationship

(noun) | The way in which things are connected. | *After the Revolutionary War, the **relationship** between Britain and America changed.*

relative to

(adj. phrase) | Compared to. | ***Relative to** my interest in sports, my interest in computers is high.*

constant DAY 1

(adj.)   Going on without stopping; not changing.

*The **constant** sound of lapping waves soothed me to sleep.*

consistent DAY 2

(adj.)   Always behaving the same way or having the same ideas.

*Because the teacher is **consistent** in his expectation, the students know what to do.*

consistency DAY 3

(noun)   The act of behaving the same way or having the same ideas.

*His **consistency** on the field led his teammates to count on his winning plays.*

consistency DAY 4

(noun)   The thickness, stiffness, or firmness of something; texture.

*The **consistency** of the glue was too thin, so the cardboard pieces just slipped off each other.*

conform

(verb) To act in a way that agrees with a rule or standard.

*His shirt must **conform** to the school dress code.*

correspond

(verb) To be in agreement with or match something.

*The birds I see in that nest **correspond** to the ones pictured in this book.*

corresponding

(adj.) In agreement or matching with.

*Fill in the bubble with the **corresponding** letter of your answer.*

correspond • correspondence

correspond

(verb) To write to another person.

*I **correspond** with my grandmother who lives in Brazil.*

correspondence

(noun) Communication in writing.

***Correspondence** by letters is no longer practiced by most people.*

distinct

(adj.) Clearly different from someone or something else.

*This puppy's **distinct** markings separate it from the others in the litter.*

distinction

(noun) A feature or mark that makes someone or something different from another.

*There is an important **distinction** between scanning a story and reading it closely.*

differentiate

(verb) To find or see differences or distinctions between things.

*I can **differentiate** between a cube and a square.*

discriminate

(verb) To see a clear difference; to make a distinction.

*With her telescope, she can **discriminate** between the two planets.*

represent • representative

represent

(verb) To stand for or be a sign of something.

*The blue ribbons I won at the state fair **represent** much hard work.*

---

representative

(adj.) Being an example of a group or kind.

*Chandler showed the class a **representative** sample of his seashell collection.*

representative

(noun) A person or a thing that is typical of a group.

*The visitors to the zoo watched the snake, a **representative** of the reptile family.*

symbolize

(verb) To stand for or represent something else.

*In this story, the kites **symbolize** the free spirits of the people.*

symbol

symbol

(noun) Something that stands for or represents something else.

*The olive branch is a **symbol** of peace.*

---

symbolic

(adj.) Acting as a symbol.

*The handshake is a **symbolic** gesture of goodwill.*

determine

DAY 1

(verb) To decide or settle an issue or matter.

*The election will **determine** our representative on the student council.*

determine

DAY 2

(verb) To find out by watching and checking; to discover.

*Doctors **determine** how well the medicine is working by examining the patients.*

determine

DAY 3

(verb) To bring about; to be the cause of.

*The amount of light and water will **determine** how well the plant grows.*

influence

DAY 4

(verb) To have an effect on someone or something.

*The behavior of older children **influences** younger children.*

(noun) The effect of someone or something.

*Researchers are studying the **influence** of air pollution on our health.*

respond

(verb) To reply or give an answer.

*The students **respond** in unison to the teacher's questions.*

response

(noun) A written or spoken answer or reply.

*Peter's **response** to Mr. Kowal's question was polite and to the point.*

elaborate

(verb) To add details to something or explain more fully.

*Your story would be more interesting if you would **elaborate** on the character description.*

elaborate

(adj.) Complicated; detailed.

*The design for the treehouse is **elaborate** because it includes shutters and window boxes.*

category   DAY 1

(noun) A class or group of things that have something in common.

*I place books about history in one **category** and biographies in another.*

categorize   DAY 2

(verb) To place or arrange things into categories.

*I **categorize** my photos by event.*

consist   DAY 3

(verb) To be made up or formed.

*The art show **consists** of works created by middle school students.*

constitute   DAY 4

(verb) To form or make up.

*Grades nine through twelve **constitute** the high school.*

Daily

Grades 1–8

Language
Review

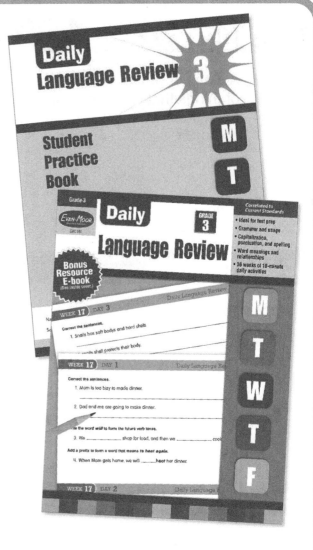

*Proven effective in **improving** students' **language skills!***

Students practice grammar, punctuation, usage, and sentence-editing skills using the research-based model of frequent, focused practice.

- Students complete half-page activities on days 1–4 and a more extensive full-page activity on day 5.

- Includes a detailed scope and sequence, skills list, and home–school connection projects.

136 pages. Correlated to current standards.

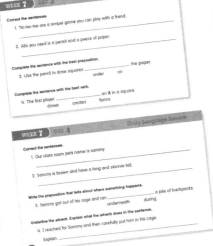

Better | Together

Complements the skill practice in:
Language Fundamentals